6-24-03.

TO OLIVER :

I'm asking EMILY & SARAH
TO READ THIS TO YOU SO
you will be the best
dog EVER!

**Mordecai Siegal and**

**Matthew "Uncle Matty" Margolis**

# Solutions

## For Your Dog
## —and You

Simon & Schuster

New York   London   Toronto   Sydney   Singapore

SIMON & SCHUSTER
Rockefeller Center
1230 Avenue of the Americas
New York, NY 10020
Copyright © 2001 by Mordecai Siegal and Matthew Margolis
All rights reserved,
including the right of reproduction
in whole or in part in any form.
SIMON & SCHUSTER and colophon are registered trademarks of Simon & Schuster, Inc.
Designed by Karolina Harris
Manufactured in the United States of America
10   9   8   7   6   5   4   3   2   1
Library of Congress Cataloging-in-Publication Data
Siegal, Mordecai.
Solutions for your dog and you / Mordecai Siegal and Matthew Margolis.
p.   cm.
Includes bibliographical references (p.   ).
1. Dogs—Behavior. 2. Dogs—Training. 3. Dogs. I. Margolis, Matthew. II. Title.
SF433 .S575   2001
636.7'0887—dc21       00-053341
ISBN 0-684-86472-X

# Contents

# Solutions

# *Introduction*

*hy* can't a dog be more like a human? Wouldn't it be wonderful if the family friend could take himself out for a walk, use the toilet and flush it, stay off the couch when his fur is loose, know when not to jump on you, cut down on his food when he gets too paunchy, and sit down and talk things over when he's troubled? Dogs do none of these things and everybody knows that. It's a question of language. So why do we put up with all the difficulties, misunderstandings, and questions that arise in dog ownership? The answer to that is far simpler than trying to understand why people couple up or have children.

Given half a chance, everybody loves a dog. With

the blink of an adoring eye and a fuzzy face in the palms of the hands, millions of dogs become part of millions of families on a regular basis. A dog, any dog, can plunder the human heart in three short beats and keep it long after he spends his last scent. It is open-heart surgery without so much as a break in the skin. The explanation for this canine version of cardiac arrest is simple: A dog loves you with no questions asked. If you treat him right you could be Quasimodo, Iago, and Lucifer himself rolled into one gargoyle and he would still lick your hand and jump with joy every time you come home.

It is this unique blessing of unconditional love and the appeal to our parental instincts that motivates most dog owners to tolerate stubbornly the entire catalog of difficulties and dilemmas that eat away at the edges of our pleasure. Most dog owners, especially the new ones, have concerns about their family pet that may include keeping him healthy, getting him to listen to you, stopping him from peeing on the floor, taking him to work or another city, leaving him home, getting him to eat sensibly, or even saving his life. There are virtually hundreds of bewildering situations one may encounter when living with a dog. It is important to understand that almost everything that is disturbing about a dog's behavior is usually related to getting him to adjust to life among the humans. All the rest has to do with dog sense that is both common and uncommon. What you need are solutions. Solutions for your dog—and you.

Most dog owners don't know Shih Tzu from Shinola.

What they need is information they can put to use about day-to-day concerns, including the mysteries of dog behavior and training. This is important for experienced dog owners as well as first-timers. Life with Fido can be easier with the insider information offered here that translates dog dilemmas into solutions. The advice we offer represents our combined experience and accumulated knowledge as well as our understanding of what dogs and dog owners need to know. Within these pages are suggestions, tips, and tutorials in a clear, concise, easy-to-use format that should answer most questions about living with a dog. Our solutions are also drawn from experts such as those at Matthew Margolis's National Institute of Dog Training, veterinarians, breeders, groomers, and other dog professionals, as well as research from respected sources.

*Solutions: For Your Dog—and You* is divided by subject and presented in what we consider to be a logical order of need for most dog owners. For example, the first chapter is "Love for Sale," which is important to people who are considering getting a new dog. Throughout the book each subject is broadly presented in a short explanation and then solutions are offered for each aspect of the topic. In some instances the solution offered may be lengthier than usual given the demands of the subject matter, such as obedience-training techniques. The table of contents offers a list of all the topics that are covered and should be sufficient to help you navigate your way to the solution you need. We hope this book helps you and your dog become happier with each other.

# One

# *Love for Sale*
## (Getting a Dog)

*G*etting a dog is easier than ordering movie tickets on the Internet. All you have to do is walk past a pet shop or pull a telephone tag off a notice in the supermarket. There are always neighbors over the back fence trying to sell you or give you a puppy. And then there are the shelters and rescue organizations and newspaper ads all with tempting offers. You can just sit back and let it happen, or you can be smart and learn how to do it properly. If you want to live with a dog successfully you should try to learn all you can about dogs, especially those breeds in which you are most interested, before you bring a dog home. It is essential that you choose the right dog—a completely individual matter. No one can tell you which is the best kind of dog for you or which one will make you happy. That is a decision only you can make. The two most important factors to consider are the dog's health and temperament. Obviously, you want a dog with no health problems and a dog that will not bite you or those around you. If the person selling you a dog says, "It's just business, nothing personal," walk away. Your choice is nothing but personal.

### The best dog for you

Since you are about to make a twelve- to fifteen-year commitment you need to be sure you make the right choice. Here are some important questions you need to consider for yourself:

- Gender: Do you want a male or a female?
- Size: Do you want a large, medium, or small dog?
- Age: Do you want a puppy, adolescent, or adult dog?
- Where you live: Do you need a dog that is best for the city or the country?
- Time available: Do you leave the house to go to work or do you stay home?
- Your expectations: Do you want a pet for companionship or a pet that protects you?
- Activity level: Do you want an athletic dog or a couch potato?

Getting a dog is a very personal choice. Consult a dog book that illustrates all the different breeds, delves into their histories, and enlightens you about what they were bred to do. Go to dog shows to see the breeds up close and determine if one of these is going to be the new member of the family. Talk to breeders and exhibitors at dog shows or at their kennels to get an experienced point of view. Talk to a professional dog trainer. Ask a veterinarian about potential medical problems inherent in your chosen breed. Visit local rescue shelters and dog pounds and consider one of their dogs. You will be saving his life. Do your homework before taking a dog into your life so that you make the right choice. Remember that this is for the entire life of the dog and for a large part of your own life. The most important rule of thumb for selecting a dog is: Do not select the puppy, but the dog you think he will grow into. All puppies are cute and adorable, but within a year they become adult dogs. Think about that.

### Getting one dog or a pair of dogs at the same time

If your heart is set on having two dogs, you should consider getting them one at a time. That will give you the opportunity to get to know each dog individually and prevent them from bonding with each other instead of with you. Even though your puppies may be from the same litter, they will still have personality and, possibly, gender differences. Most dogfights occur between dogs of the same sex. For that reason, get dogs of the opposite sex to avoid problems of that type as they mature. Bear in mind that raising two puppies at the same time is a lot of work.

### *Getting a dog from a breeder, a shelter, a rescue organization, or from a pet shop*

There are different reasons to go to each of the above places. Eliminate going to a pet store because of the source of the dogs and the quality of the animals. If you want a purebred dog or if you are interested in showing dogs, select a dog from a reputable breeder. Many breeds have their own rescue organizations that are involved with finding good homes for unwanted dogs of their specific breed. Be sure to get information on the dog's background and past history, especially as it pertains to health and temperament issues. There are some great dogs in shelters, and you just need to learn how to pick out the best dog for you. It is important to find out as much of any dog's background as possible to determine if the dog has any specific behavioral problems.

#### HOW TO SELECT A REPUTABLE BREEDER
- Seek out a vet for recommendations.
- Contact the American Kennel Club or the United Kennel Club for referrals to a breeder.

#### HERE ARE SOME QUESTIONS TO ASK A BREEDER
- How long have you been breeding dogs?
- Are your puppies socialized to people and familiar noises?
- May I meet the puppy's parents?
- Does the breed have any health issues?
- How healthy is the puppy? His parents?
- Is there a guarantee for health or behavioral defects?

A good breeder will ask you many questions to be sure you will provide a good home for his or her puppy.

### YOU SHOULD VISIT THE BREEDER AND INVESTIGATE

- Is the kennel clean?
- Are the puppies perky and friendly?

Use common sense. If the breeder doesn't seem like a good choice, chances are he or she is not a good choice.

### GUIDELINES FOR CHOOSING A DOG FROM A SHELTER

- Before you leave home, discuss and write down the type of dog you would like to have in your family (size, age, and whatever else is important to you).
- Walk slowly and look carefully at each dog.
- Make a second pass as you begin to narrow down the choices. Write down all the dogs that you have selected.
- Walk through a third time and concentrate on the dogs that you wrote down.
- Ask the shelter attendant about the dogs you have selected. Ask as many questions as you can think of about their history, why they are there, housebreaking, personality, training, if any.
- Spend some time with each of your choices.
- The final step in the process is to have your new dog examined by a veterinarian, although many shelters have all of their dogs examined before letting them go. However, if your own vet finds a

serious health problem with your new dog it is not unreasonable to return the dog.

### What to look for when getting an older dog

Get as much background and history as you can. Has the dog had any formal training? Depending upon where you purchase him, a private home or a shelter, it may be difficult to get any background information. Try to determine the dog's personality. Is he shy, aggressive, stubborn, timid, even-tempered? Ask important questions, such as whether or not he has lived with children. What is the reason he is up for adoption? You must make sure that he is going to fit into your home and your life. Why not have him evaluated by a professional dog trainer to be sure he is the right dog for you. That is what you would do before buying a car or a new home. Why not a dog? Most dogs are loving and affectionate, so you must not confuse an excitable dog with a bad dog. It's just a matter of obedience training. Some dogs are shy or aggressive. It is very important for you to determine which is okay for you and your family. Shy dogs can make wonderful pets; they just need a lot of loving and a gentle touch. There are different types of aggressive behavior in dogs, and it is very important to have such a dog evaluated by a dog trainer or behaviorist to see if he is a good dog for you.

### *Choosing a male or a female*

This is a matter of personal preference. Male dogs are usually larger than females and eat more. They often require more effort to train, or at least require firmer handling. Male dogs are more likely to wander off, especially if there is a female in heat in the area. They are more prone to getting into fights with other male dogs. Males are usually friskier and more difficult to handle. Female dogs are, as a rule, smaller in size than males and a bit more compliant and less excitable. They are almost always easier to handle and train. Female dogs go into heat twice a year, for approximately three weeks. During this time the animal secretes an odorous fluid intended to attract male dogs for the purpose of mating. Of course, all of these sexual characteristics, in both males and females, can be eliminated entirely by having your male or female neutered, which is highly recommended. Male dogs are castrated and female dogs are spayed. These procedures prevent unwanted mating, pregnancy, and the resulting puppies. It also calms most dogs and solves some behavioral problems such as aggression, wandering, or inappropriate sexual conduct. If you plan to have your dog neutered, choosing a male or female dog is simply a matter of personal preference.

### *Puppies versus older dogs*

If you like babies and want all the cuteness, sweet smells, and the licking that a baby dog gives, and if you want to be the first owner, then puppies are for you. It is probably best to get a puppy at the same time you have a baby so they can grow up together, if you can handle all the work involved. The down side is that puppies require a lot of care, time, and effort. It's like having a new baby in the house, and you must be able to fit this into your life-style. A puppy is a twenty-four-hours-a-day, seven-days-a-week responsibility, for at least the first ten months. Getting an older dog offers many advantages, depending on how you live. In most cases an older dog is already trained, and all the annoying puppy behaviors such as teething, chewing, nipping, and all the rest are gone. You can see what the dog is going to look like as an adult, because he is already fully grown. An older dog will not necessarily need constant attention, as a puppy would. It is a myth that you can't bond with an older dog. Older dogs are just as lovable as puppies and bond just like puppies. With either, though, you are guaranteed a loving and affectionate companion for the life of the dog.

#### THE BEST AGE TO BRING HOME A PUPPY

The best age for a puppy to go to a new home is between eight and twelve weeks. By then he has been with his mother and siblings long enough to develop the skills that he needs to help him in the big world. If he remains with the litter past that time, he begins to accept his rank in the social order and may become too submissive or too aggressive. At eight weeks he is old enough to adapt to a new home and a new family. He is also highly trainable for the basics at this age.

### THE SUPPLIES AND EQUIPMENT YOU NEED TO BUY BEFORE BRINGING A NEW PUPPY HOME

- a book on puppy care
- a dog crate and a dog bed
- two puppy collars (a flat nylon collar and a training collar)
- one six-foot leather leash
- an identification tag
- water and food bowls
- stain remover and scent remover
- chew toys, preferably made of synthetic materials
- premium dog food, formulated for puppies
- a natural bristle brush and a medium-fine comb

# Two

# How to Get Your Dog to Love You
## (Bonding)

*T*o bond with your dog is to establish a relationship with him that is based on love and friendship. It is exactly the same idea as bonding with a child. Once a bond has been established it will last forever, barring any extreme negative behavior or circumstance. Bonding is the pairing of two or more individuals who develop a long-term attachment to each other as the result of shared experiences. Through the course of their lives they strive never to lose each other.

### The importance of bonding

Bonding is the most effective way to establish a successful relationship with your dog. It opens the door for the best part of dog ownership, unconditional love.

Bonding is the most important first step to managing your dog properly, which helps enormously to develop a long-term, loving relationship with him. Bonding is also the first necessary step toward successfully training your dog.

### Bonding with an adult dog

Age does not matter. What is important is your attitude; it makes all the difference. By treating your dog like a new member of the family and giving him all your love, you will feel like you have lived with him all your life, even if it's been less than a week. A dog purchased at three years of age can offer you the most wonderful experience of your life as if he were a puppy. It is simply a matter of bonding properly with him.

### Bonding with an adopted adult dog

The question sometimes arises as to whether or not a dog will bond with a new person after having lived with someone else. Suppose you adopt a dog that came from a family that gave him up. Will he always be thinking about his first family and searching for them, or will he become a member of your family? If you bond with him properly and give him the affection, friendship, and care he deserves, he will probably love his new family as much as the old one, or maybe more.

### Introducing your new puppy to the family in order to bond successfully with him

Everyone bonds with his or her dog differently. Each member of the family should take the time to develop a personal relationship with the new family

member. There are many different ways of relating to
a dog, and that's what makes each family member's
bond unique. Some people are more demonstrative
with emotions than others, and that's okay. The most
important thing is that everyone in the family spends
some exclusive time with the dog and expresses as
much affection as possible. Everyone has his or her
own way of expressing affection, and no member of
the family will relate to the dog in the same way. That
means the dog will relate differently to each person,
too. You should expect this. It is important that everyone accepts the new dog as a member of the family
and finds a way to establish a relationship with him.
Anyone living in the house should make an effort to
bond with the new dog on some meaningful level.

### How bonding is accomplished

Every day that you have positive interaction with
your dog, you are bonding with him. The perfect formula for bonding is to treat your dog with love, praise,
and affection. You must never yell at or hit your dog,
because these things either prevent a bond from developing or tear apart a bond that has already been established. Among the various ways to bond are feeding,
walking, playing, petting, talking to, grooming, or enjoying quality time with your dog. All dogs crave physical contact with their families. These things are an
important expression of your love and feelings for
your dog. Be as extravagant as possible with your
physical expressions of endearment. Nothing establishes the bond quicker than letting your dog know
how you feel about him.

## Bonding techniques for puppies and adult dogs

Puppies and adult dogs respond beautifully to the same bonding techniques. For example, when you feed your dog, be affectionate and tell him what a good dog he is. Touch him and pet him. Look at him and talk to him and don't be afraid to give him a hug. The same applies when going out for a walk. Brushing, combing, and bathing are wonderful opportunities to touch the dog lovingly and tell him how much you like him. Take him with you frequently on errands and when you go shopping. Take the dog with you while doing household chores. Exercise and play are important bonding opportunities to interact with the dog in a happy, enjoyable way. Throw him a ball, a stick, a Frisbee, or any toy he likes, and play games. Always be positive with the dog, and don't be afraid to get down on the floor to his level and play with him. Roll over with him, hug him, and hide his toy only to let him find it under you. Make sure your play activity involves cuddling and hugging. Anything that allows you to interact with your dog in a loving, positive way is a bonding technique and therefore important.

## Bonding with a second dog

Do not allow a new, second dog to bond exclusively with the other dog in your house. This is important if you want a relationship with the new dog that is interactive with you. You can avoid this mistake by spending the first two weeks with the new dog alone at least half of the time, without the other dog present. Dogs tend to relate to their own species easier than with humans if given the choice. You can create a much more social, happier, and certainly more trainable pet by getting your dog to bond with you first.

### The effect of bonding on dog training

Bonding with your dog is crucial to training. Once a loving relationship is established, most dogs become very willing to please their owners, and obedience training thus becomes much easier. You do not need special skills to bond with your dog. All you need is a big heart and a willingness to express your feelings to your dog. Training requires knowledge, but bonding requires love. A loved dog is a happy one. Being happy becomes a normal state for such a dog and is shared with anyone who comes in contact with him. Bonding is the first important step to take before training your dog.

### How the bond is affected when you leave the dog behind on a business trip or vacation

Once you have established the initial bond with your puppy or adult dog, it lasts for a lifetime. Leaving the dog behind for a few weeks does not harm it. It does not matter. Dogs do not seem to have a sense of time. For this reason you get the same greeting from your dog whether you are gone for one hour or one week.

### Bonding to those outside the family

Can a dog love everybody else the way he loves you? Here is the surprising answer: no. Dogs do love many people in different ways, but as his owner you have a special bond that cannot be duplicated. The wonderful thing about a dog is that he will accept any kind of relationship you want, provided it is based on kindness and love.

### The time it takes to bond with a dog

It may take as little as one day or as long as three weeks. The more you interact with your dog on a daily basis, the more quickly the bonding takes place.

### Who the new dog will love the most in a family

Dogs do not love equally. Whoever spends the first two weeks loving, caring, and spending the most time with the dog will be his master. He will love other members of the family but on a different level. There is usually one person who provides most of the dog's needs and is the one who will develop the strongest bond. For this reason it is best to divide responsibilities for the dog as much as possible. It is amazing how fast a bond can be established when someone does just one thing for the dog on a daily basis.

## *Three*

# *Where Do I Start?*
## *(Choosing a Training Method)*

*N*o matter how much you holler or hit, beg or plead, bribe or threaten, you will never get a dog to listen to you without training him. Dog training involves teaching your dog when he may and may not respond to his impulses and how to perform simple tasks such as sitting or lying down or holding a position on command. But that is quite a lot to get from a dog, and it comes about only from obedience training. Training a dog is the only answer to living with one. The ability to train dogs is a very special skill, for it requires a person who not only loves dogs but understands them and knows how to teach them to be responsive to human commands. Obedience training teaches a dog how to live successfully in a human environment with dignity and pride as a member of a human family. It is no small thing. By training a dog you teach him and his family how to develop a full relationship based on canine pack behavior. There are a number of methods and formats for training dogs, and there are many available dog trainers. The effectiveness of any training method depends on the dog, the person, and the circumstances, not necessarily the method itself. As for dog trainers, some are good at it, some are truly gifted, and some have no aptitude at all. Once you understand that your dog must be trained you must decide on the type of training to use, and then select a good method. There are four different sources of training from which you can choose:

1. self-help books and videos
2. classes of ten to twenty dogs, in which the dog's owner must work with the dog in each session
3. private training sessions, which are usually given in the home
4. board-and-train kennels where the dog is left for a number of weeks or months and then returned to the owner upon completion of the training

The following information should provide a solution for you.

### TRAINING THE DOG YOURSELF

| *Advantages* | *Difficulties* |
| --- | --- |
| • The cost is very low. | • It requires a serious, un- |

- You may enjoy training your own dog.
- You will feel pride in the accomplishment.
- You can set your own pace/schedule.
- This is a wonderful way to bond with your dog.

failing commitment to complete the training once you start.

- You must be consistent about how you train your dog.
- You must set time aside every day and conduct the required sessions without fail.
- You must be willing to study the training book you choose carefully or the videotape from which you work.
- You must be patient. A dog in training can tax your patience.

## Training Classes

### *Advantages*

- Its low cost.
- You are trained how to train your dog.
- You will be socializing with other people and dogs. This is fun and beneficial for you and your dog.

### *Difficulties*

- Many problems that happen in the home cannot be solved in a class format.
- Dogs of all different ages and learning abilities are taught the same way. This would be like having kindergarten through high

school in the same class, teaching one level to all the students at the same time. It is a one-size-fits-all approach.

- Dog fights can occur.
- There is minimal personalized training.

- Only one family member can train the dog in the class. It is very important for the whole family to participate in the training process.

## PRIVATE TRAINING

### Advantages

- One-on-one training is the format. A private trainer trains the dog and then teaches the owner how to use the training.
- A private trainer works with the entire family, in the home.
- Problems that arise in the home and surrounding areas—such as going to the vet,

### Difficulties

- The lessons are scheduled at your convenience.
- Engaging the services of a private trainer is considerably more expensive.
- Commitment to the training must be made without neglect.
- The dog may be prone to listen more to the trainer than the owner.

walking on a leash,
and running in the
park—are addressed
and worked on.

### BOARD AND KENNEL TRAINING

*Advantages*

- The dog comes home fully trained.
- Training is accomplished faster and more efficiently. At a training kennel the dog is trained six days a week.
- The dog is socialized with other people and dogs.
- The dog is trained with and without distractions in a controlled environment.
- Professional trainers teach you how to handle the dog.
- This format offers greater convenience for the owner. Many dog owners leave the dog in the kennel for training while they go out of town or on vacation.

*Difficulties*

- This is the most expensive way to have a dog trained.
- The dog is away from home for at least six weeks.
- The dog is exposed to a kennel environment.

## How to find a dog trainer

- Get a referral from friends and neighbors with a good experience.
- Ask your veterinarian for a referral or check his or her bulletin board.
- Look in the yellow pages and talk to at least three or four trainers before making a choice.
- Go on the Internet and use a search engine.
- Check with a local shelter.

## Questions to ask the dog trainer

- How long he or she has been in business?
- If it is a company, how many trainers do they have?
- What method of training will be used on your dog? (They should train dogs with love, praise, and affection. The dog should never be hit, yelled at, or punished. Good trainers do not treat the dog inhumanely. Bear in mind that this is a member of your family and you are sending him to school to learn, not to be abused.)
- Does the company or individual trainer have a business license?
- What types of courses are offered?
- Is the training facility clean?
- Have any of the trainers published articles or books?
- Do they specialize in one breed only or do they train all breeds?
- Will they allow you to tour the facility?
- Do they welcome calls from the clients while the dogs are in training?

- If you use a board-and-train facility, how often are you invited to visit the dog?
- Check the referrals of past clients.
- Do they offer obedience training as well as problem solving?

## REASONABLE EXPECTATIONS FROM A GOOD DOG TRAINER OR TRAINING FACILITY

- Your dog should be in a clean, wholesome, social environment that has a positive atmosphere.
- The dog trainer should be skilled and fully qualified, offering your dog a loving, positive experience.

# Four

# *He Won't Listen to Me/He Won't Do What I Tell Him to Do*
## (Training Your Dog Yourself)

*T**here** is no more important solution for most be-havior issues than getting your dog under control. As you walk him down the street you do not want a four-legged whirlwind dragging you along like debris in a class-two hurricane. Nor do you want your dog sniffing around where you or your friends do not want him to sniff. For as many dogs that live with people, that is how many different reasons there are for getting the family pet under control without having to place him under house arrest. This is a job for dog training and dog train-ing alone. Here, then, is a pretty fair, though concise, course in canine obedience training. If your dog is completely untrained, you can follow the entire section in the order it is presented, or you can select any of the various solutions to try out or tailor to your needs. Help yourself. We suggest you start from the beginning and work your way to the end. Either way, enjoy.

### *Why you should train your dog*

Training helps remove the emotional obstacles that stand between humans and their dogs. If a dog is trained properly, he will probably behave well and cause few problems throughout his life. A good definition of training is teaching a dog to respond properly to humans and to do what is expected of him when a command is given. All dogs can be trained. The secret ingredient to successful dog training is affection.

### *The proper frame of mind for training a dog*

There can only be one relationship in dog training. You are the teacher and the dog is the student. Dog training involves a set of specific techniques that have been proven to work time and again. There is no guesswork involved. In order to train your dog successfully you must learn the techniques and how to employ them.

When training your dog, do not allow yourself the luxury of becoming angry or impatient with your lovable student. It is unfair and inaccurate to assume your dog is the problem. Your attitude should be the same as if you had a child in nursery school. In the beginning all a child or a dog can do is show up. All the rest depends on the teacher, who in this case is you.

### Hitting your dog

Hitting your dog with your hand, with a rolled-up newspaper, or with any object will cause your dog to fear you, or worse. He could become aggressive and start fighting back. Hitting your dog, like hitting your child, creates aggressive behavior and an attitude about aggression. It has nothing whatsoever to do with teaching. A dog that is hit in the course of obedience training does not learn anything except to dread your presence. Think about your hand as an object of love. Ask yourself if it is possible to feel good after hitting your dog.

### Those who should participate in the training process

Everyone who becomes involved with the dog on a day-to-day basis can and should participate in the training. The more the merrier. If you want a great relationship with a dog and expect him to listen, you should participate in the training. It is not only fun, but also rewarding. All the kids, relatives, and friends living in the same house will love being able to control the dog in those situations where control becomes necessary. There is a great satisfaction in giving a dog a reasonable command and having him comply. Dog training is fun.

### The length of each training session

Depending on your dog's personality and age, training sessions should take place once or twice a day lasting a minimum of fifteen minutes or a maximum of forty-five minutes. Older dogs have less tolerance and patience, and puppies with a shorter attention span are more easily distracted. Some dogs are extremely hyperactive, while others are quite lethargic. These variables set limitations on how long and how often you can train your dog. The number of training sessions a day and the time duration of each one must be dictated by the individuality of your pet.

### *Dog training methods*

The best method is customized dog training. There are at least six different personality types, and a dog may possess as many as five of them in combination:

- high energy
- strong-willed
- shy/insecure/timid
- calm/easygoing
- (dominant or fear) aggressive
- responsive

It is not too difficult to determine your dog's personality type if you have paid careful attention to his behavior.

You should adapt your training techniques to your dog's specific personality. For example, if your dog is shy of loud noises, you should always use a soft tone of voice rather than a harsh tone. On the other hand, if your dog is high energy or strong-willed, a firmer tone of voice should be used. Tailoring your use of training techniques to your dog's temperament or personality is the best method for success.

### Where to train your dog

Training should always be done in a quiet, secluded area. Your backyard or inside your home when no one is there are the most ideal places for obedience training sessions. The fewer distractions the better. Once your dog has mastered the command you are teaching with no distractions, the next step is to expose him to obeying around the very set of distractions that will occur in his world.

### The importance of your voice in training

The sound of your voice and its intonation are two key elements in enjoying successful training, as well as in developing a positive relationship with your dog. A dog's hearing is approximately five times greater than human hearing. If you raise your voice in anger, your dog will react with fear because his hearing is sensitive to loud sounds. If you use a moderate, loving tone of voice when training your dog he will want to please you.

### The importance of your body language

Our bodies communicate messages to our dogs as meaningfully as words. A good working philosophy of body language for dog owners is to be as nonthreatening in manner or gesture as possible. For example, if your dog is small, do not stand so close that you tower over him, forcing him to crane his neck to see you. It is better to kneel next to him so that he can relate to you with ease and comfort. Do not make sharp, angry moves as you train your dog with his leash in your hand. Sudden or jerky gestures also have a negative effect on a dog. As a matter of fact, a normal, easy manner is always best when training your dog or for doing anything with your dog.

### Staring directly into your dog's eyes

Harsh looks and direct stares into your dog's eyes are not a good idea. If your dog is shy or timid, you will intensify his submissive behavior. On the other hand, if your dog is dominant, you will increase his level of aggressiveness, which can, in turn, induce a hostile action such as barking, growling, or even biting.

### Your dog is afraid of hand movements

Most dogs enjoy food treats. Every time you approach your dog with your hand, extend it with a treat in your palm and allow him to see it, sniff it, and then slurp it into his mouth. As he takes it, praise him and tell him what a good dog he is. If your dog likes a ball or specific toy, repeat the same action with that. Eventually he will associate your hand coming toward him with something pleasant and loving. Your hand should only be used as a source of love, praise, and affection. Hands must be for loving only.

### The equipment you will need to train your dog

Dogs more than twenty pounds require a six-foot leather leash that is 5/8 to 3/4 inches wide, for training as well as everyday use. Dogs under twenty pounds require a leash six feet in length and half an inch wide.

We refer to collars used for training as *corrective collars*, which are mistakenly referred to as *choke collars*. You may buy one in nylon or metal, depending on the age, size, and breed of your dog. For example, long-coated breeds such as Afghans, English Sheepdogs, or Collies should work with a nylon collar so that it does not rub the fur away around the dog's neck. Short- to medium-coated breeds can tolerate a metal corrective collar. It is always best to use a metal corrective collar when appropriate.

### Holding the leash properly

With the corrective collar around the dog's neck and the six-foot leash attached to it, stand with the dog to your left as you both face the same direction. Open your right hand and hook the loop at the end of the leash over your thumb. Adjust the length of the leash by gathering up the slack and holding it in both hands.

### The right and wrong way to put on the training collar

#### THE RIGHT WAY

When you put the corrective collar on the dog's head and he is facing you, it should form the letter P for perfect. If you jerk the leash, the collar will tighten around the dog's neck and release smoothly when you relax it.

#### THE WRONG WAY

The collar will form the number 9 and will not release at all after jerking and then relaxing the leash. It will remain tight around your best friend's neck.

### Communicating with your dog even though you don't speak the same language

There are many ways to communicate. Your voice is certainly one of the most important aspects of communication. One-word commands, the volume and tone (harsh, soft, loving, etc.) of your voice all communicate in a direct way to any dog. The various aspects of bonding are significantly important when it comes to communication. Bonding is a form of communication involving touching, feeding, body language, and expressing the way you feel about the dog. You can even sing to your dog as a means of communication. All of these are everyday interactions that establish the relationship between you and your dog. A major form of communication is obedience training. The various techniques of dog training are all about learning how to communicate with your dog.

### Punishing your dog

Please don't. Accept the dog training philosophy that asks you to teach and praise your dog, not punish him. Please remember that punishment does not teach anything except fear. Once your dog learns a command and he fails to respond to it properly, you should correct him with any one of the correcting techniques offered here. They are not meant as punishments but rather as ways of communicating to the dog that he didn't do what he was supposed to do. Think of dog training as a positive form of teaching. Whatever the situation, teach and correct.

## *Teaching your dog the training commands*
### Leash correction

Hold the leash with both hands a bit below waist level. Jerk the leash sideways and slightly upward to the right. As you jerk the leash say "no" in a firm tone of voice. Return to the original position in one quick motion. It is important to give the dog verbal praise immediately after each correction.

### Leash breaking

Many dogs refuse to walk when attached to a leash for the first time. Resistance to the leash may be expressed in three different ways: by the paws, the mouth, or the teeth. If a dog thrashes at the leash with his paws or bites it, say "no" in a firm tone of voice and pull the leash away. Do not forget to praise your dog after the voice correction. If your dog refuses to walk while on the leash, kneel and call him to you in a happy, loving tone of voice. When the dog finally comes to you, praise him lavishly. Try to create a pleasant association with the leash.

### Sit

Kneel on the right side of your dog. Grasp the hip joints or hip sockets of your dog, which are at the base of his spine. When you feel two indentations, press them firmly, but gently, with your fingers. Tell your dog "sit" stretching the word out, as in "S-i-i-i-t." While you say "sit," use your hands to guide him into a sitting position by pushing down on his hips with your left hand and at the same time pulling the leash up with your right hand. As you stretch the word out, adjust the pitch of your voice to sound cheerful, gentle, and reassuring. Once your dog is in the sit position, praise him enthusiastically even though your hands helped him. Repeat this procedure until the dog begins to sit on your command without the use of your hands.

Teaching "sit" is likely to be the first command you're going to teach your dog. It is the beginning of the teacher-student relationship. It establishes you as the leader. From this command your dog will learn all others.

### Sit/Stay

With the dog on your left side, both you and the animal should face the same direction. Give him the command to sit. Praise him after he goes into the proper position.

Teaching the hand signal. Give your dog the command to stay! A hand signal must accompany the verbal command. Hold the leash with your right hand and allow enough of it to drape across your knees so that there is a little slack. Give the hand signal by flattening your left hand and keeping all fingers straight and close together, as you would if you were swimming. Give the command "stay" while placing your left hand about four inches in front of the dog's eyes. Be careful not to touch his eyes with your hand. The hand signal must be given quickly so that it blocks his vision for only a second. Return your left hand to your side instantly after blocking his vision with it. The dog will soon associate the hand signal with the verbal command "stay." Eventually, the dog should remain in the stay position with the use of the hand signal only.

### The pivotal turn on the left foot.

This is an essential part of the teaching technique for stay. The goal is to make a pivotal turn so that you face the dog without stirring him. The point is to teach him to hold his position as you move in front of him while saying the command "stay." To accomplish this, use your left foot as a pivot and do not move it from its original position. Step off with your right foot and turn to face the dog. Allow your left foot to rotate in place as your right foot moves forward one step so that you eventually face the dog. At the same time that you turn around, keep the leash above the dog's head, holding it to one side so that it does not hit him on the chin. Keep the leash tight enough to restrain the dog's movements. If you do this in any other way the dog will assume you are about to move forward and start to go with you.

As you turn your body, place your right foot on the ground and move your left foot next to it. You have now made a complete turn and are facing the dog. Lower the leash slightly, but keep it tight. Stand in front of the dog for about thirty seconds while he remains in the stay position. Praise him generously in a calm, soothing voice for his correct response. The pivotal turn is merely a teaching tool and need not be used after the dog has learned the command completely.

The goal is to teach him to remain in sit/stay from a

distance of three feet until he is released from the command. Slowly back away about three feet from the dog. While holding the leash above his head, shift it to your left hand, placing your thumb inside the loop at the top. Grasp the main line of the leash about halfway down with your right hand. Hold it loosely directly under your left hand. The leash should be able to slide freely through the right hand as you back away, allowing it to extend. This will prevent any slack from developing as you move.

Back away from the dog slowly and gently. Allow the leash to slide through your right hand as you move backward. The dog may begin to walk toward you as you move away; if he does, say "stay" and move toward him. Pull the leash through your right hand as you move forward and hold it once again above his head. Stepping toward him will stop him from moving. Praise him once he has stopped moving. Pause for several seconds and then begin backing away again until you are three feet away. Praise him once you reach the desired three feet and hold the position for thirty seconds. Repeat the process fifteen times.

Back away six feet from the dog and repeat the procedure as above. Continue walking backward slowly one step at a time. After each step, remind the dog to stay, and praise him for doing so. At some point during this gradual backing away from him, the dog will probably jump toward you. When he does, you should command him to stay and simultaneously step forward to block him, shortening the leash through your right hand, holding it tautly above his head for control. As soon as he sits down, praise him generously, pause for several seconds, and then begin backing away again until you reach the full limit of the leash. From that distance, remain standing in front of him for thirty seconds. Practice this command at least twelve times.

## Heel

Attach the dog's collar and leash. Standing to his right, gather approximately one third of the leash in your right hand, while the remainder of the leash hangs between your hand and his collar. Both arms should be relaxed.

Say your dog's name, followed by the word "heel," emphasizing the command word. The word "heel" is an action command requiring forward motion. Your dog's name is a signal alerting him to watch you and prepare to move. As you say the command word "heel," step forward on your left foot, which is closest to the dog and will get him moving the instant you do.

Allow your dog to run ahead of you. As he gets to the end of the fully extended leash, grasp it with both hands and administer a leash correction. Stop walking forward. Make a fast U-turn, and as you do, say the command heel in a firm tone of voice. Walk briskly in the opposite direction. The dog will have no choice but to turn and walk in the same direction as you.

As he approaches you, pat your thigh to encourage him to come close and praise him when he reaches your side. After a correction, your dog may approach and then run past you. Should this happen, begin this exercise again.

### AUTOMATIC SIT

The goal is to teach your dog to sit automatically whenever you are out for a walk and you decide to stop. Give your dog the command heel and begin to walk at a moderate speed. After a minute or two, slow down gradually, which in turn will get your dog to slow down, too. Stop completely and give the command sit. Kneel or bend over your dog by his right side, depending on his size. Gently grasp his hip joints or hip sockets, and press them firmly but gently with your fingers. Tell your dog "S-i-i-i-t," stretching the word out on the vowel sound. While you say the command, use your hands to guide him into a sitting position. As you push down with your left hand on his hips, pull the leash up with your right hand.

Once the dog is in the sit position, praise him lavishly, even though you placed him there. Repeat this procedure until the dog begins to sit automatically each time you stop.

### DOWN

Place your dog in the sit/stay position on your left side, and face the same direction as the dog. Hold the leash with both hands in the proper position. It should extend upward from the dog's collar across your left thigh to your hands, which should be in the center of your body near your waistline. By not allowing any slack in the leash, you will prevent him from squirming or playing. If he tries to move away, tighten the leash, give him the command sit, and then praise him. Now proceed to teach this command. The following two techniques, the hand technique and the paws technique, are offered as a matter of choice, so that if one does not suit your dog you can try the other. After employing either one of these techniques, continue the training with the front technique.

### The Hand Technique

Stand at your dog's side; kneel down next to him if he is small. Flatten your left hand and close all your fingers together. Raise your left hand slightly above the eye level of the dog and to the right of his head making sure there is no slack in the leash. Your fingers should be pointing frontward.

Say the command "down," and lower your left hand toward the ground. In doing so, the flat of your palm will hit the top of the leash about where the clip connects to the collar. The verbal command should be stretched on the vowel sound as you lower your hand as well as the pitch of your voice: "D-o-o-w-w-n."

When your palm reaches the dog's neck, press down on the leash at the collar. Unless your dog is very large, the downward pressure from your palm will push him down, into the proper down position onto the floor or ground.

Through his peripheral vision your dog can see your left hand push him into the down position, which he will associate with lowering his body to the ground. This is also how he learns to respond to your proper hand signal. Repeat this procedure at least fifteen times, or as many times as necessary to lower the dog without any resistance.

### The Paws Technique

Kneel at your dog's right side and face the same direction. Give him the commands for sit and stay.

Praise him each time he obeys. While kneeling on your left knee, give the command "down," drawing it out softly on the vowel and dropping your pitch as you pronounce it: "D-o-o-w-w-n." Gently hold the dog's two front paws with your left hand so that they do not get pressed painfully together.

As you give the verbal command, gently lift the dog's front paws off the ground and pull them forward and downward until they reach the ground. This takes away his support, which gently causes him to decline into the down position. Repeat this action fifteen times or until he goes down with almost no resistance at all.

### THE FRONT TECHNIQUE

After completing either the hand technique or the paws technique you must continue with these next two techniques for teaching down.

This is an important step in reinforcing your dog's knowledge of the hand signal.

Now that he has learned to be pushed into the down position by your hand from the side, it is safe to assume that you can do it from the front. With the dog in the sit/stay position, turn about-face and stand in front of him. Hold the leash taut and slightly above his head with one hand and raise the other hand with your fingers extended straight and close to each other.

Lower your hand onto the leash and push it downward. Accompany this with the verbal command "down." As your voice stretches and lowers in tone, the dog is once again pushed to the ground with the pressure applied to the leash from your hand. At this point it is likely that your dog will drop down by himself. If he does, praise him enthusiastically and then repeat the exercise fifteen times. In any case, praise the dog the instant he is all the way down each and every time.

### The Front Technique from a Greater Distance

Place your dog in sit/stay. Get in front of him, standing as far back from him as he can tolerate without moving; with some dogs the distance will be two feet, three feet, or perhaps six feet. Hold the leash with your left hand and tighten it slightly above his head if he tries to move away. Raise your right hand straight up with the fingers close together. Give the verbal command "down," stretching out the word and using the descending tone of voice.

Lower your right arm as you say the verbal command. Allow the flattened right hand, palm down, to land on top of the leash. Continue pressing down until both the leash and the dog touch the floor. Praise the dog for going down into the proper position. Repeat this procedure fifteen times, or until he drops to the floor without resistance.

An important next step is to repeat the entire front technique from a greater distance but do not touch the leash with your hand as your arm is lowered. Allow your hand to brush past the leash without actually touching it. This will be exactly the way your hand signal will look from a distance once your dog has learned to respond perfectly to the command. Repeat this phrase until he obeys the down command perfectly from both your verbal command and hand signal.

### DOWN/STAY

With the dog on your left side, both you and your dog should be facing in the same direction. Give him the command to sit; praise him. Give him the command "Down"; praise him.

Next, give your dog the command to stay. The hand signal as previously instructed in sit/stay accompanies the verbal command "stay." Hold the leash with your right hand and allow enough to drape across your knees so there is a little slack. Give the signal with your left hand, flattening it and keeping all fingers straight and close together. As you give the command "stay," place your left hand about four inches in front of the dog's eyes, careful never to touch them. The hand signal is accomplished quickly and should block his vision for an instant. Return your left hand to your side quickly after blocking the dog's vision. Your dog should eventually remain in the stay position with the use of the hand signal exclusively after constant repetition of this action.

#### The Pivotal Turn on the Left Foot

The goal here is to make a pivotal turn so that you can face the dog without him moving out of position. Maintain the hand signal in front of the dog's eyes throughout the following motion; use the left foot as a pivot and do not move it from its original position. Step off with your right foot and turn to face the dog.

Allow your left foot to revolve in place as your right foot moves forward one step so that you are almost facing the dog. At the same time that you turn around, keep the leash above his head, tight enough to restrain the dog's movements. It keeps the dog from moving. If you do this in any other way he will assume you are about to move forward and will start to go with you.

After you have placed your right foot on the ground facing the dog, move the left foot next to it so that you have accomplished the complete turn and are now facing him. Stand in front of the dog for about thirty seconds while he remains in the stay position, and praise him generously for his correct response. The pivotal turn is merely a teaching tool and will not be used after he has learned the command completely.

Slowly back away until you are approximately six feet in front of the dog. The goal is to teach him to remain in the down/stay position from a distance of six feet until he is released from the command. Shift the leash to your left hand, placing the thumb inside the loop at the top. With your right hand, grasp the main line of the leash about halfway down and hold it loosely under the left hand. As you back away, the leash should be able to slide freely through the right hand, allowing it to extend to full length. This prevents any slack from developing as you back away.

Start backing away. The leash slides through your right hand as you hold it firmly with your left, and gets longer as you move backward. The dog may begin to walk toward you as you move away. If he does, give him the verbal command "stay" and move toward him. Pull the leash through your right hand as you move forward and hold it once again above his head.

Stepping toward him will stop him from moving, and once he stops moving he must be praised. Pause for several seconds and then begin backing away again until you are six feet away. Praise him once you reach the desired distance and hold the position for thirty seconds. Repeat the process fifteen times.

### COME WHEN CALLED

Place your dog in a sit/stay position. Back away from him slowly until you reach the full extent of the leash. Face the dog from a six-foot distance and give him the verbal command "Okay, Eddie, come." Draw out the "o-k-a-a-y," raising the pitch of your voice cheerfully. The verbal command always has three words: "Okay, Eddie, come."

As you say "okay," simultaneously do two things: Summon the dog to you by quickly moving your extended right hand to your chest and pull the leash toward you with your left hand. Finish the command: " . . . Eddie, come."

#### Teaching the Hand Signal

The verbal command is always accompanied by a hand signal. The hand signal helps eliminate any confusion for your dog if he is called from a distance. It is based on the common gesture that is used to summon a friend or a child from a long distance. The right arm hangs at the side of the body and is raised in a turning, leftward motion as though it were wrapped around a large object.

The entire command for the purpose of this lesson is as follows: "Okay . . . (Pull the leash with your left hand. Raise your right arm and swing it around to your left side. Complete the gesture and return it to its natural position) . . . Eddie, come." As soon as you have given the hand signal, place your right hand on the leash, using it with the left hand in a hand-over-hand motion to pull the leash in like a rope. By the time your dog reaches you, five feet of leash should be gathered in your hands. Praise the dog. Practice this procedure at least fifteen times.

### AUTOMATIC SIT

Place the dog in the sit/stay position and walk backward to the end of the leash. Hold the leash high with your left hand, permitting just a little slack, and say "okay, Eddie, come." When you say "okay," give the hand signal with your right hand, but do not pull on the leash. As soon as you have given the hand signal, put your right hand on the leash, using it in a hand-over-hand motion to pull in the leash, and gather in all but twelve inches as the dog comes to you.

Holding the remainder of the leash up high with your left hand, command the dog to sit as you pull up on the leash, maneuvering him into the sit position. Praise him lavishly. Repeat this procedure until he gets it right at least fifteen times.

### PLACE

At your command the dog stops whatever he is doing and leaves wherever he is doing it, walks to a designated place (such as a corner of the room), and stays there after given the command to stay. Place involves a verbal command and a hand signal.

First, decide where you want the dog's place to be

located. It is most often on the floor in a corner of a room, such as the kitchen. Do not make the dog's place in the same room where you dine, because that gives him the opportunity to beg for food. You might even use a dog crate (with the door open at all times), a dog bed, a pillow, or a blanket to help establish the place and also to make it comfortable. Once you establish your dog's place you can now train him to go there on command. This could become the most frequently used command of all if you have a busy household.

Go to the side of the room opposite from your dog's place, and place the correction collar and leash on him. Position yourself next to the dog's right side, facing in the same direction, as you would in the heel position. Hold the leash taut in your left hand, about twelve inches above the dog's head. When giving the verbal command, use a cheerful yet firm tone of voice.

Say "Domino, place." Using your left foot, walk the dog briskly to his place, turn around with him at your side, and come to a full stop. Praise him for going there.

Then give him the command to sit, and praise him. Then give the command "Down," and once again praise him. Say "stay" using the proper hand signal as taught earlier. Praise him, drop the leash, and walk to the other side of the room. If he tries to get up or leave the position, use a voice correction, "No." If he goes back to his down position, praise him. If he does not, repeat the down and stay commands, praising him after each. If he holds the down/stay position for thirty seconds, call him to you, using the proper come when called command, "Okay, Domino, come." When he comes to you at the other side of the room and sits in front of you, praise him lavishly. Repeat these instructions at least fifteen times, and then take a five-minute break.

Repeat the procedure again, but from another room. Repeat the procedure at least fifteen times.

From here on teach the same procedure but from greater distances and other rooms of the house. Start leaving the room after placing the dog in down/stay for longer periods of time. Extend the down/stay time for one minute, two minutes, and so on. When you can give him the command and he leaves the room and goes to his place in another room, plops down, and stays there until you release him with the command "Okay" or "Okay, Domino, come," your dog has learned the command "Place."

# Five

# *Myths of Dog Ownership*

**A** *myth* is as good as a mile when it comes to living with a dog. There are many misconceptions about what our four-legged friends are really like and how we should treat them. Here, then, are the most common canine fallacies that continue to interfere with a happy dog life. We hope to set the record straight.

### *Big dogs need more exercise than small dogs*

This is not true. All dogs need exercise. The extent of that need is determined by the breed and the temperament of the dog rather than the size. Some breeds are highly active and energetic and need to work off their energy no matter how big they are. This is especially true of terriers and hunting breeds. It's true, size is not important. Find out what function your dog's breed was meant to perform, and that insight will help guide you to his exercise requirements. Ask any dog professional (such as a vet, a trainer, or a groomer) about your breed's original function or purpose. It is amazing how many toy breeds are sensitive and highly energetic with a lot of steam to work off. Conversely, a number of large breeds are lethargic, do not move very quickly or energetically, and limit the amount of exercise they will tolerate. English Setters, Saint Bernards, and Basset Hounds are among these breeds. An extremely active and energetic dog will require a good run, some play time, and several walks a day to keep him fit no matter how big or small he is. The truth is that all dogs require exercise.

### Dogs can be spiteful or jealous

This is not true. What does a spiteful or jealous dog look like? These are human characteristics. Spiteful behavior is a form of revenge characterized by animosity and deceitful behavior, possibly based on anger and resentment. Dogs are far less complicated than that and much nicer. Much of a dog's behavior is based on his immediate response to what is directly in front of him. Dogs that appear to be spiteful are really being aggressive or defensive as a direct response to something that disturbs them. Jealousy is much too sophisticated an emotion for the simple, direct mental processes of a dog. Some dogs may appear to be jealous because they want more attention, but this is not the same as human jealousy, in which people feel extremely upset by other people. When a dog acts in what appears to be a jealous manner and also acts aggressively, he is being territorial and protecting what's his. Is that jealousy or something else?

### Dogs feel guilty when they do something wrong

They do not. When a dog looks guilty because he did the wrong thing chances are he is anticipating a harsh or negative response from you learned from past experience. Of course there is no way to know for sure if a dog experiences the human characteristics of guilt such as anxiety, anger turned inward, and self-criticism. What do *you* think? Perhaps you're the one feeling guilty because you left him alone all day or forgot to walk him.

### It is cruel to have a big dog in an apartment

Not at all. Dogs are among the most adaptive creatures in the animal kingdom. Believe it or not, their families are the most important element in their lives. When a dog is cared for with love and affection, fed properly, given good health care, and obedience trained, he has it made. It really doesn't matter if he lives in the country, the suburbs, or a big city. Exercise and training compensate a great deal for living in a small apartment or in less than ideal conditions. Dogs are not into real estate. They are into loving care. Of course, a romp in a field or a dip in a lake is always welcome.

### You have to hit your dog to correct him

No, no, no, a thousand times no! Never hit your dog for any reason, not with your hands, not with a rolled-up newspaper, not with *anything*. If you want the love and attention of your dog, you must develop a bond between you in order to create a relationship based on trust. How are you going to create a trusting relationship with a dog if you hit him? Why would your dog trust you if you swatted him with a rolled-up newspaper for doing something that he can't understand in the first place? When training dogs, you must correct them in order to communicate that they did something incorrectly or failed to obey. There are several approaches to correction, but they are all techniques for communicating an idea rather than punishment or retaliation. Corrections in dog training may involve the quick snap of a leash and collar, the use of a noise-maker, a stern vocal response, or combinations of the above. You must never hit your dog to correct him. It doesn't accomplish anything except to make him fear you, which is not the basis of a loving relationship.

### Knee your dog in the chest or step on his hind paws to keep him from jumping up on you

This is wrong. It is never a permanent solution to the problem. It teaches your dog nothing except to fear you or to associate you with pain. But why would you want to physically hurt your dog in the first place? What if you have a toy dog? Do you hire a small person to do the kneeing? This is only one of several physically abusive practices believed by far too many dog owners to solve a behavior problem. Hurting a dog has nothing to do with teaching. As in all dog training and behavior problems, the tried and true techniques that have been developed are the most effective and humane ways of addressing the issues.

### *Rub your dog's nose in his own mess to housebreak him*

This practice is not only abusive and disgusting, but is the least effective way to deal with a dog's failure to be housebroken. Plain and simple, it does not work. A dog's body waste is a means for communicating with other dogs, for claiming territory, for finding a mate, for establishing a place in the social order of a pack. It is much more than the aftermath of a meal. It is not only unkind to rub his nose in his stool or urine, it is a violation of his nature. It is difficult enough for a dog to come to terms with the fact that he is not allowed to eliminate where he feels he should. But using a primary behavior as a form of punishment is counterproductive and destructive to his good nature and desire to please you. Learn the proper way to housebreak your dog with the use of tried and true techniques and forever put aside the chamber of horrors of so-called dog training.

## *Your dog will be happier if he is free to roam around your house rather than confined to one place*

A young, untrained dog who is allowed to roam freely from room to room, especially when no one is home, has the potential to get into serious mischief and cause a great deal of damage to the house and harm to himself. Unconfined dogs may chew up furniture and clothing, defecate and urinate on beds and carpeting, and knock anything and everything over out of curiosity, restlessness, boredom, loneliness, or even teething pain. In addition to the harm a free-roaming dog can do to your home, he is also a danger to himself. He might chew on an electric cord and seriously burn himself. He might pull something down that scalds him or breaks a bone. He might swallow poisonous cleaning products or prescription drugs or plastic bags, all of which can create a life-threatening situation. The solution lies in prevention. Do not allow a young or untrained dog to roam freely around the house. Confine the dog to one room or place him in a spacious dog crate when you are not home to watch him.

## *You have to wait six months to train a puppy*

Not so. You can start training a puppy as young as seven weeks, and that training includes housebreaking, problem solving, and obedience training. Of course, training a very young puppy requires much gentler handling, greater patience, and more time with each command. A dog's ability to learn begins very early. As a matter of fact, a seven-week-old puppy is at his most adaptive at that age and therefore easier to train.

### You cannot teach an old dog new tricks

Actually, you can start teaching a dog as old as twelve years of age or as young as seven weeks. A dog is almost never too old or too young to learn.

### A wagging tail means a happy dog

This is not true. A wagging tail can also mean your dog is excited, nervous, or even aggressive. A wagging tail is not necessarily something to jump for joy about. Most of the time, however, when your dog wags his tail he is feeling good about something, or perhaps begging, or anticipating a good thing.

### There are certain breeds that are vicious (such as Rottweilers or Pit Bulls)

Absolutely false. There are no bad breeds. There is bad socialization, bad breeding, bad living conditions brought about by bad dog owners. A dog becomes dangerous because of these things and not because of his breed characteristics. Even the word "vicious" is misused when it comes to dogs. The word implies an intent to be cruel or bring harm. A dog may be dangerous because he is either defending himself or protecting what he thinks is his and for no other reason. Sometimes very small dogs from traditionally benign breeds can hurt someone in a serious way. It is not about breeds.

# Six

# *Bones of*
# *Contention*

**N***ext* to housebreaking, feeding your dog is the greatest concern for new dog owners. What to feed, how to feed, eating behavior, and all the accompanying problems are the subjects of this section. To the modern dog the food chain pertains to a string of supermarkets and not which species eats which. As far as feeding is concerned, dogs never had it so good. Some people prefer to cook for their dogs, while most people take advantage of the tremendous array of high-quality dog food that is available. And yet many dogs do have eating problems. Here are a few of the problems that exist and their solutions.

### Your dog drinks out of the toilet

There are three reasons for this: The dog is thirsty, or the lid is up and he is big enough to reach in, or he is bored. The solutions are to leave him more water, close the lid, give him more play time and exercise. Oh, yes. Close the door to the bathroom.

### You leave water out for your dog all day long

There are pluses and minuses to leaving water out all day. If your dog is outside during hot weather, it is absolutely necessary. If your dog is indoors all the time, he does not need water all day. Making water available every three or four hours is sufficient. He should definitely get water after each meal. You must take into consideration your dog's special needs, which could involve medication or extreme thirst. Too much water could lead to housebreaking accidents.

### You've changed your dog's food and now his stomach is upset and he has developed diarrhea

It is important to know that most dogs have very sensitive stomachs and a sudden change of food will cause problems. If the problem already exists, put your dog on a bland diet for a couple of days with a small quantity of cooked chicken breast mixed with white rice or cottage cheese, several times a day. Once the diarrhea is gone, resume your dog's regular diet. To avoid having this problem again, you must slowly change the dog's diet over a four-day period by adding one-fourth of the new food to three-fourths of the old food on the first day. Each day thereafter, increase the new food and decrease the old food by fourths until the dog is eating the new food entirely. This is a proven formula that works for most dogs.

### You feed your dog table scraps

It is not a good idea for several reasons: It can upset your dog's stomach, it can ruin his desire to eat his own dog food (which is best for him), and of course it will get him to develop bad eating habits. Don't feed your dog table scraps unless you want him to be an annoying beggar. You may think it's cute and loving, but other members of your family or your dinner guests may not like it. Once the dog begins this habit he cannot figure out who likes it and who doesn't. If you want a happy, healthy dog, make him stick to his own food in his own bowl.

### You've noticed that some dog breeds and some individual dogs require a higher protein diet than others

The very active hunting and working breeds require more protein in their diet if they actually hunt or work. The same is true if a dog is outdoors most of the time, especially in cold weather. Puppies, pregnant dogs, nursing mothers, some emotionally stressed dogs, and dogs that work require a high protein content in their diet. A happy dog, living indoors, with no real work thrives on what dog food manufacturers refer to as a "complete and balanced diet." Ask your veterinarian for the specific nutritional requirements of your dog.

### You're not sure if canned or wet dog food is better than dry dog food

Which is best? This is a personal choice based on individual requirements. The answers to the following questions should help you decide: Does your dog prefer wet or dry dog food? Maybe he would prefer a combination of both. Does your dog get enough water in his diet? If not, a canned food consists of approximately 74 to 78 percent moisture; dry dog food contains approximately 10 percent moisture. Canned dog foods are usually more expensive; dry food is usually more economical. Dry food does not spoil as quickly as wet food does once the can has been opened. Wet or dry, it is important to read the contents label and determine if it contains sufficient nutrition for your dog. Consult a veterinarian for this information. If you use a premium brand dog food, both wet and dry will satisfy your dog's needs.

### Your dog seems allergic to some kinds of foods, as humans are

Some dogs develop a food allergy, which appears in the form of a skin disorder. Typically, though, a dog with a food allergy usually suffers with other allergies as well. The skin rash is almost always aggravated by severe scratching and biting at the points of irritation. It can also be accompanied with digestive upset. You must consult a veterinarian for this condition, who will probably prescribe a hypoallergenic diet as well as treat the rash topically.

### You're worried that you aren't feeding your dog enough (or too much)

Here is a typical feeding schedule that has proven to be more than sufficient for most dogs. Puppies from three to six months old should be fed three times a day. Youngsters that are six months to one year old should be fed twice a day. Adult dogs one year and older should be fed once a day. Some vets recommend that all adult dogs should be fed twice a day. The feeding schedule should be set according to your dog's age, size, state of health, and energy level. Here is a set of general guidelines for the energy requirements of an average adult pet dog, with the daily number of calories necessary in your dog's food to maintain optimal body weight:

| If your dog weighs (in pounds) | Feed him (in calories per day) |
| :---: | :---: |
| 2 | 125 |
| 4 | 205 |
| 6 | 280 |
| 10 | 410 |
| 15 | 555 |
| 20 | 690 |
| 30 | 935 |
| 40 | 1,160 |
| 50 | 1,370 |
| 75 | 1,860 |
| 100 | 2,305 |

Bear in mind that these guidelines do not apply to puppies, adolescent dogs, seniors, hardworking dogs, high-energy dogs, pregnant or lactating females, or dogs with various medical problems. Since no two dogs have the same ability to absorb nutrients from the same quantity of food, a good rule of thumb is to feed him an amount that best maintains his optimal body weight. Find out from your veterinarian what your dog's ideal body weight should be and try to maintain it.

### Your dog seems bored with his regular food

Some people believe that dogs should eat the same thing every day. There are those whose greatest pleasure is to pamper their dogs and give them a great variety of food. Who is right? Dogs do better on a consistent diet that is the same every day. Some of you may not like that answer, but a dog's stomach is very sensitive and can easily become upset from extreme changes in the diet or gourmet foods that are too rich. Table scraps and frequent between meal treats can spoil your dog's appetite and, in addition, upset his stomach. And then there are the picky eaters. Variety is no help for them. Of course your dog's appetite may fall off now and then, and that is not necessarily a problem unless it is persistent, accompanied by signs of illness or weight loss. This requires the attention of a veterinarian. If your dog loses interest in his food, try moistening his dry dog food with either warm water or broth.

### You've heard that some foods are not good for your dog, and others are actually dangerous

Chocolate rarely harms humans but can be dangerous for dogs because of a caffeinelike ingredient called theobromine. Chocolate is poisonous for dogs. Onions and garlic also can cause serious medical problems for dogs, resulting in anemia and other blood disorders. There are a number of foods that produce an allergic reaction in dogs with a predisposition to be allergic, and among these are milk, horsemeat, and eggs. Some rich foods, table scraps, gravies, spices, and excessive fat also can give a dog digestive problems. Other foods to avoid feeding your dog are most dairy products because they can be difficult to digest (with the exception of cottage cheese). To insure that your dog is safe, stick to a regular diet of dog food.

### Your dog has swallowed something poisonous

The ASPCA National Animal Poison Control Center at (800) 548-2423 is available to handle emergencies twenty-four hours a day, seven days a week. There is a charge payable by credit card. Veterinarians and toxicologists are available for consultation. For nonemergency information about pesticides that affect animals and humans there is the National Pesticide Telecommunications Network (NPTN) at (800) 858-7378. The service will answer most questions concerning pesticides and how they affect animals and humans. It is available from 6:30 A.M. to 4:30 P.M., Pacific Time, seven days a week.

### *Your dog drinks out of the swimming pool*

Although it is not a healthy practice, your dog will probably survive drinking from the swimming pool. However, swimming-pool cleaners containing chlorine or muriatic acid are caustic acids with a pH below 2.0 and when consumed directly will cause serious injuries that are life threatening. Swimming pool cleaners are in the same category of toxicity as antirust compounds, toilet cleaners, gun-cleaning solutions, and battery acid.

### *You avoid feeding your dog before he exercises*

You should feed your dog at least two hours before you exercise your dog in order to avoid a life-threatening condition called gastric dilation-volvulus, more commonly referred to as *bloat*. The condition primarily affects large-breed, deep-chested dogs such as Great Danes, German Shepherd Dogs, Saint Bernards, Irish Setters, and Doberman Pinschers, among others. The affliction takes place shortly after the dog eats. It occurs because of an accumulation of air and fluid in the stomach that cannot be expelled by belching or vomiting. The condition is characterized by a distension of the stomach or intestines, which may twist and then rupture. Death often ensues. For dogs that survive this condition, frequent, small meals are recommended and dry food should be moistened. Eating and drinking before exercise is definitely not recommended.

## *You give your dog treats as a reward during housebreaking training*

This is a no-no during housebreaking training. It is very important to stay on a strict feeding schedule. Giving treats will break the schedule and cause piddle-poo accidents. After housebreaking, however, you may give your darling dog between-meal treats as long as you don't turn him into a four-legged barrel.

## *You go to work in the morning and leave food down in the kitchen all day for the dog*

This is referred to as a self-feeding routine and of course requires the use of dry dog food along with a large bowl of fresh water. Moist food will spoil within an hour or two and semimoist food may create more thirst than your dog's water supply can provide. Self-feeding is fine for dogs that eat only what they require and leave the rest for later. There are those dogs that wolf down as much as they can all at once and simply eat too much. This form of gluttony can only create an obese dog that will have a short, unhealthy life fraught with medical problems. If your dog is not obese or prone to gluttony you may make dry food available at all times. Otherwise, feed him once in the morning and again when you get home from work.

### *Automatic self-feeders*

These are wonderful devices for dogs whose family is not home during the day. Some are electrically timed and automatically provide a ration of food at preset times. Others are simply upside-down self-feeding containers that work by gravity. As the dog eats and empties the space containing the food, more dry food drops down and keeps replenishing the ration. Here, too, the caution about obesity applies as referred to previously. If your dog is prone to wolfing everything down at once, eating as much as you make available, or has an obesity problem it is best to avoid the self-feeding container. Many dogs like the attention of being fed. It creates a ritual that lets the dog know you care. Thus, self-feeders can be alienating.

# Seven

# Housebreaking

**W**hen it comes to housebreaking, an ounce of prevention is worth pounds and pounds of cure. The prevention part is the training, and the cure pertains to all the floor and carpet cleaning you will not have to cope with. Puppies piddle like a summer sprinkle but adult dogs pour like a spring shower. Either way, a dog with housebreaking problems creates an unpleasant mess. More dogs alienate their families because of their housebreaking problems than for any other reason. The primary solution for all housebreaking problems is to first learn what housebreaking really means and then use a proven housebreaking technique in order to train your dog properly.

### What is housebreaking?

A definition: Training your dog or puppy to pee and poop outdoors, on a schedule you determine. The dog must always control himself until he can be taken out. Once the dog has been trained to do this he must never relieve himself indoors. Housebreaking does not in any way involve the use of newspapers on a floor in your home. To successfully housebreak your dog, please see "Develop a housebreaking program for your dog" below.

### Develop a housebreaking program for your dog

SCHEDULE

| Time | Activity |
| --- | --- |
| _____ | Walk |
| _____ | Feed, Water, Walk |
| _____ | Water, Walk |
| _____ | Feed, Water, Walk |
| _____ | Water, Walk (last water of the day) |
| _____ | Walk |

### Suggested schedules

These schedules should only be used during the training period. Afterward, they can be adjusted according to your individual needs, the age of your dog, and the advice of your veterinarian as it pertains to your pet's nutritional requirements.

### For puppies seven weeks to six months:

| Time | Activity |
| --- | --- |
| 7:00 A.M. | Walk the dog. |
| 7:30 A.M. | Feed, water, and walk. |
| 11:30 A.M. | Feed, water, and walk. |
| 4:30 P.M. | Feed, water, and walk. |
| 8:30 P.M. | Water and walk (last water of the day). |
| 11:30 P.M. | Walk the dog. |

### For puppies six to twelve months:

| Time | Activity |
| --- | --- |
| 7:00 A.M. | Walk the dog. |
| 7:30 A.M. | Feed, water, and walk. |
| 12:30 P.M. | Water and walk. |
| 4:30 P.M. | Feed, water, and walk. |
| 7:30 P.M. | Water and walk (last water of the day). |
| 11:00 P.M. | Walk the dog. |

### For dogs twelve months and older:

| Time | Activity |
| --- | --- |
| 7:00 A.M. | Walk the dog. |
| 7:30 A.M. | Feed, water, and walk. |
| 4:30 P.M. | Water and walk. |
| 7:30 P.M. | Water and walk (last water of the day). |
| 11:00 P.M. | Walk the dog. |

### For dogs belonging to those who leave for work (any age dog):

| Time | Activity |
| --- | --- |
| First thing in the morning | Walk the dog. |
| Before leaving for work | Feed, water, and walk the dog. |
| Midday | Have someone come in and feed, water, and walk your puppy. (Only water and a walk for a grown dog.) Use a friend, relative, neighbor, or hired person to do this. |
| Home from work | Walk the dog. |
| Early evening | Water and walk the dog (last water of the day). |
| Before bedtime | Walk the dog. |

Always walk your dog outside or let him use the backyard. You must stay with your dog to assure elimination.

Walk your dog for twenty minutes. If he does not relieve himself, bring him inside and either confine him or watch him very closely. If you catch him going to the bathroom, correct him and take him outside right away to finish.

Repeat the walk if necessary one hour later.

### Diet

Food requirements vary, depending upon the breed, the environment, exercise and stress factors. Since each product varies, read the suggested daily feeding guides on your food package or consult your veterinarian. *Leave food down for fifteen minutes. Do not leave food or water down at all times during housebreaking.*

### Odor neutralizer

Wash all areas where the dog has gone to the bathroom with an odor neutralizer. Follow directions on the label or container of the product.

### Confinement

Your dog should be confined when you are not home or when you are unable to watch him. Confine him with a mesh puppy gate or wire dog crate only. Do not expect your dog to understand the use of a dog door until he is completely housebroken.

- no accordion gates
- no tying him down
- no confinement behind closed doors
- no confinement in isolation such as the basement or in a garage

### Correction

Correct the dog only when you catch him in the act of eliminating. Say "No," in a firm tone of voice, take the dog outside immediately, and praise him when he eliminates there.

SPECIAL INSTRUCTIONS
- Never hit your dog.
- No snacks during training.

- Do not correct your dog unless you catch him in the act.
- Be aware of the water content in the food you are using.
- Puppies generally have to eliminate at these times:

  - first thing in the morning
  - immediately after a nap
  - immediately after eating and drinking
  - immediately after exercise

Housebreaking can be completed in as soon as three days or as long as two weeks, depending on the dog and his owners. Setbacks are rare and usually are connected to the owner's issues. Some dog owners are forgetful or too busy to maintain the schedule, indulge their dogs' whims and desires when it comes to training of any kind, or simply do not take the training techniques seriously. Housebreaking a dog requires diligence, consistency, and determination.

### You've heard that you should rub your puppy's nose in his own mess when he has a housebreaking accident

Everyone has heard at one time or another that rubbing your dog's nose in his own mess is the best way to teach him not to "go" on the floor. The question is whether or not this really works, because whenever you try to teach him the lesson, he runs the other way and you have to chase him all over the house. Obviously he doesn't like it, because he runs the other way. This type of owner discipline easily can be considered barbaric. Attila the Hun was probably the first one to use this alleged technique. Ultimately, all you are doing is scaring your dog to death, in addition to robbing him of his dignity. More significantly, you are damaging the existing bond between you. Rather than punish the dog in this nasty way, you must learn how to correct your dog for his mistakes and consider what the reason is for the accident. For example, his stomach could be upset, his schedule for going out may be erratic, or he could be improperly confined. You are advised to learn the proper way to housebreak your dog using teaching methods that really work.

### *Your puppy messes in his kennel whenever you leave him alone*

There could be several reasons for this. He may not be on a proper feeding and walking schedule. You may be leaving him confined for too long a period of time for his age. For example, a puppy should not be left confined for more than four hours at a time. Another possibility is that he is being overfed or given too much water.

### *Your dog will not sleep through the night and has to go outside*

What do you do if your spouse gets so angry about this "middle of the night" problem, and says, "We might as well have a baby in the house"? Well, the truth is you do have a baby in the house. This particular housebreaking problem usually develops because the dog is on an improper schedule. The rule should be no more than seven to eight hours between the last walk at night and the first walk in the morning. Of course that depends on the age of the dog. If you have a puppy under six months, you may have to get up a little earlier, but a dog six months or older should be able to make it through most of the night without going out. Another reason for the problem could be feeding and giving water to the dog too close to his bedtime. A dog's last drink of water should be at approximately seven o'clock at night and the last meal should be given at approximately six o'clock in the evening.

### You're not sure how often to give your dog water during housebreaking

This depends on the life demands of the dog's family and the environment they live in. If you are home all day, it is sufficient to give your dog water every four or five hours, but his last water should be at seven o'clock. If you are not home all day and you have a fenced-in yard, your dog should have access to water all day long. If you are gone all day and you do not have a yard, provide a pet sitter or dog walker throughout the day. Finally, if your dog is alone all day and there is no one to walk him, then you have no choice but to leave water down all day long.

## Your dog continually relieves himself in one room of your house, usually on the same spot

There are several reasons why this is happening. If it is in an area where you started housebreaking with newspapers on the floor (which is called paper training) and then switched to taking him outdoors (which is housebreaking), he may be going back to his old way of doing what you essentially taught him to do. Even though newspaper is laid down, you are still teaching your dog to relieve himself on the floor. Another reason has to do with his being drawn back to the odor of his previous release. Some dog experts have found that a dog can smell one part urine to one million parts water. One solution is the use of an odor neutralizer, which can be purchased from a pet supply store or mail-order catalog. Another solution is to restrict him temporarily from that one area of your home. Depending on whether this is a urination or defecation problem (or both), you may have to adjust his feeding-watering-walking schedule.

## Crate training is not working

Suppose your puppy came from a pet shop, and before that from a puppy mill, a common situation for many new dog owners. That means he was raised in a cage all of his life until you brought him home. As you can imagine, your puppy's life was not too pleasant, and there may be many bad associations with being in a wire dog crate. This is a difficult problem. If you live in a home with a fenced-in yard or have a dog run, enclosed patio, or terrace, it is probably better to leave him outside all day, if he is old enough and if the weather is not severe. Make sure the dog has as much water as he needs. He will begin to learn that going to the bathroom outside is okay. This should take no longer than a week to resolve. The alternative is to confine your dog in one room, such as the kitchen, with a see-through mesh gate.

### Your dog uses the kitchen floor to relieve himself even though you want him to go outside. He keeps returning to the newspaper left on the floor

If your goal is to housebreak your dog—and that means teaching him to go outside, never in the house—it is a mistake to paper train him first. In essence you are teaching your dog to relieve himself in your home and then praising him for it. Once he learns to do that properly you change the rules and want him to relieve himself outside. Somehow, some way, your dog probably is telling you to make up your mind. It is too confusing. Start housebreaking your dog over again and stay away from the newspaper-on-the-floor technique.

### Your dog often cannot make it all the way to the outside before he urinates. You've had to put down plastic rug runners

This could be a medical problem, depending on your dog's age. Obviously a trip to the vet is recommended. Some dogs are very excitable and present the problem of excessive wetting. See the section on exces-

sive wetting in Chapter 20, "He's Driving Me Crazy."
Maybe your dog is simply getting too much water, and
when you add excitement, you have piddling. Until
you find the right solution, get plastic runners leading
to the door.

### Your one-year-old dog will not lift his leg when he urinates. He is destroying your lawn with dead spots

The truth is that most dogs mature between one-
and-a-half and two years of age, so instead of your
lawn being destroyed, your bushes will be destroyed.
The best solution for this is to provide a fenced-in dog
run so that he can do his "business" there. The only
other practical solution is to take him out for walks
frequently. Either way you will then have a beautiful
lawn.

### You have two dogs. One goes outside to relieve himself in the same place with no problem. The other one refuses to be housebroken

This is not about sibling rivalry. This is about two
different dogs, and you cannot compare one to the
other. You must try to figure out why the other dog
isn't housebroken. Start the process over from the beginning.

### You say your dog is 95 percent housebroken

How do people come to these percentages? Why not
92 percent or 98 percent? If your dog is 95 percent

housebroken, what problem or problems do the remaining 5 percent represent? A great concept for finding a solution is to think like TV's Detective Columbo. Try to figure it out. Ask who the culprit is. Is it a second dog in the house, or perhaps someone is feeding the dog too many treats under the table? Ask where the accidents are happening (which area of the house). Maybe the dog shouldn't be allowed there anymore. Ask when it is happening, which time of day or night. This means the dog's feeding-watering-walking schedule may need adjusting. Ask about the specifics of the problem: urination, defecation, or both? Too much food? Too much water? Too much of everything too late at night? The answers to these questions will lead you to logical solutions. Your dog just may need more time following the housebreaking program at the beginning of this section.

### Right after changing your dog's diet to a higher quality dog food he developed diarrhea

Chances are the dog is messing everywhere in the house and you are wondering what you did wrong. It is important to know that most dogs have very sensitive stomachs and a sudden change of food will cause this problem. Put him on a bland diet for a couple of days, giving him food such as a small quantity of cooked chicken breast and rice. To avoid having this problem again, you must change the dog's diet slowly, over a four-day period, by adding one-fourth of the new food to three-fourths of the old food on the first day. Each day thereafter, increase the new food and decrease the old food by fourths until the dog is eating the new food entirely. This is a proven formula that works for most dogs.

### You moved recently to a new house with your male dog. So far he has lifted his leg and urinated on the wall of every room in the house and you want to know what is going on

This is a common problem. Your dog is marking his territory and saying "This is my house." This becomes especially important to him if other dogs previously lived there. He is simply covering the other dog's odor with his own. Here are some quick tips: Deodorize the house with an odor neutralizer. Do not give your dog the run of the house for at least two to three weeks so that you can correct this behavior by catching him in the act. This means keeping him confined to one room, such as the kitchen, when you are not home. Having a male dog neutered helps this problem.

### Your dog drinks out of the toilet at night

He does this because he's thirsty. A simple solution is to close the lid to the bowl. Oh, yes, provide him with a full bowl of water of his own . . . in the kitchen.

# Eight

# *The Family Dog*

**D**ogs play a unique role in family life, as responsive companions, playmates, and stimulating members of the family. They are usually impartial and without bias for or against anyone. They are loving friends who appreciate anyone who is good to them. A dog in the family may be the most valuable relative you have, because they do not judge anyone and they are completely accepting. Sometimes, however, dogs become lightning rods and the focus of family conflicts involving rivalry, jealousy, and competition for love and attention. Your dog is a sweet, innocent bystander and should never be placed in the middle of family discord. These are problems that deserve solutions, for the sake of all concerned, but especially the dog.

## *You want to decide what kind of dog is best for you and your family*

Which is best is not an important or even answerable question. Which is best for *you* is a more crucial question and it depends on what your life-style is like. The answers to several questions make it obvious as to whether or not a big or small dog is best for you. You must consider convenience, practicality, and personal taste when making this choice. For example, a person who doesn't have to rush off to a job each morning may have less pressure and more time to devote to the needs of a large dog. A small dog may require less time for its maintenance and be easier to care for by someone who must rush out each day to get to work. Living in the city, suburbs, or country certainly has a bearing on this decision. A giant dog in a tiny city apartment offers some obvious inconveniences. A very small, elegant dog requiring combing and brushing each day may not be the best one for roaming around a large woodsy piece of property. And then there is the question of protection. Do you live alone or with a family, and how will that affect your choice? These issues and questions must be addressed in order to make the best possible choice. Only you have the answers.

## *Your entire family should be involved in caring for the dog, including young children*

Everyone living with a dog should share the work connected with his best interests. Of course, adults must have the most significant role in raising and caring for the dog, even if it is only supervisory. All adults living in the house should do something for the dog so that the dog feels like he's living in a pack. Kids five and older can feed or help feed the dog, spend (supervised) time playing with him, help with the training commands by learning them, and of course, bathe and groom him. These are very essential responsibilities and the kids get the most out of living with a pet by taking part in them. Even playing with the dog has an important function and children love knowing that playing with the dog contributes to his happiness and good nature. When each person performs a role in caring for the dog, he or she develops his or her own special relationship with him.

### *Your dog sleeps in your child's bed*

Sorry, but this is not a good idea for many reasons. The dog may become territorial and aggressive and think that any of the furniture in your home is his bed. This can lead to serious problems, including nasty behavior when you decide to shoo him off. Of course there will also be dirt and hair all over the bed and the furniture. Remember, this is not your four-legged child. Or is he?

### *You are single and wonder if the dog in your life will be social with dates or life partners and children*

This is an important question if you are planning on having a family some day. The answer applies to both men and women. When a dog is raised with a single person and not socialized as it grows up, there is a danger that he will become shy or aggressive with the opposite sex. It is very important to expose the dog to every possible social situation, including those with men, women, children, other dogs, and even cats. Expose your dog to any activity where there are other people and dogs around and help him form pleasant associations with them. You will have a much happier and social animal with many rewards, including lots of good-natured fun for the both of you.

**You and your partner, both very close to your dog, are separating, and you're worried that this will have a negative effect on him. The question arises of who should get the dog**

The dog doesn't know that you are breaking up, so there is not necessarily a negative effect. We are not marriage counselors, so the decision must be a personal one. One way to handle this is to give the dog to the person who has the closest bond with him and has the most time and opportunity to raise him properly. If you cannot come to an agreement, think about shared custody.

**You wonder if getting another dog to keep your current dog company is the right thing to do, especially because you are a professional person with long, unpredictable work hours**

This is not a good idea. It will be twice as much work for you, and if you are already loaded down with other responsibilities it will add considerably to your burden. As long as your dog is well cared for and someone feeds, waters, and walks him, he will be very happy. By considering how much time and energy you have for your work and your dog, as well as taking care of yourself, you both will be healthier and happier.

### You selected a wonderful puppy and felt the two of you would bond. Now that he's home he seems to love your husband more than you do and you feel angry

It is normal to have feelings of jealousy over a dog. Bear in mind, however, that the one who pays the most attention to the dog, especially in the beginning, who spends the most time playing with him, and who takes the most care of him will develop the strongest bond. This doesn't really mean that the dog loves one person more than the other. There is no competition for love. Dogs love different people in many different ways. Hang in there and develop your own bond with the dog.

Also consider that there may be something wrong with the relationship with your spouse. It sounds like you need advice or counseling. You should never be in competition with your spouse over the dog. Maybe it is easier for either one of you to love the dog more than the marriage.

### Your wife pampers the family dog excessively. You seem to argue about this all the time. Maybe she should ease up with the dog

Sometimes people treat their dogs as if they were babies. This is especially common with puppies, small dogs, and toy breeds, because their dependencies bring out our parental instincts. We believe that you cannot be too good to your dog, but you can be too indulgent, especially when the dog is perceived as a child just waiting to be spoiled. Babying a dog is bad only when it is done to excess, such as carrying him around all day as if he were an infant and constantly feeding him treats. This can and often does create behavior problems. When a dog is pampered to the extreme he becomes overly dependent, shy, aggressive, unusually territorial, and possessive of the "doting parent." Some people pamper large dogs as well, which creates similar problems. The solution is to remember that the family pet is a dog, not a human, and should be treated accordingly. Too much of a good thing is not wise.

## Your husband is training your dog as if he's in the army. He is too firm

It is harmful only if he's yelling or scaring the dog. Some people think that you have to scare a dog to make him listen to you. Actually, the opposite is true. Your dog will come to fear you. The key to training a dog is knowledge, consistency, and love. You don't really need doggie boot camp for this.

## You're going on vacation and you don't want to leave your dog behind. Your spouse insists that the dog does not go with you

Sorry to say that your spouse is right. It is much better for your dog to stay behind. Your dog will be much happier and you will have a better time if he is taken care of responsibly by a professional boarding kennel, a pet sitter with impeccable references, or by some responsible adult such as a neighbor or relative. It is good socialization for your dog to be cared for from time to time by others. Another option would be to go on a dog-friendly trip, such as camping or going to a beach that allows dogs. Have a great vacation!

### Your family is having trouble agreeing on how to raise your dog

Consistency is the main element in raising a happy, stable, social dog. Try to imagine what it would be like for the dog if each person in the family gave him the same command in a different way, with none of them knowing for sure what they were doing. It can drive a dog crazy.

### Your dog listens to your spouse more than you or your children

All dogs need and obey a leader of the pack. Many men in the family assume that role automatically, without thinking about it. Men are often more demanding than women or children when dealing with the dog. Their voices are usually deeper and louder, and since dogs hear five times better than humans, they pay more attention. That doesn't mean the dog is necessarily trained or obedient, though. He may just be intimidated or even scared. It is important to remember that you must never yell at your dog. We suggest that you use your voice in a loving way for better results. Dogs will always respond to you with more comfort and love. You'll get more with honey than vinegar.

### You're worried about leaving your dog alone with your children

When you can finally leave the dog alone with the children depends on the age of your children and the age of the dog. Obviously, an older child and a puppy are going to be safe together. Nevertheless, a good rule of thumb for safety reasons is always to have adult supervision. Better safe than sorry.

### You're worried about your dog and your new baby

Even though your dog plays with the neighbor's children, he was not raised with children, so the question is whether he'll be okay with a new baby. This question comes up quite often. There is no hard and fast rule here. It really depends upon the personality, sociability, and age of the dog. Many questions regarding these factors need to be asked. Please have your dog evaluated by a professional trainer. This is very important. The safety of your baby is involved.

### You're thinking of getting a second dog but you're not sure whether to get another of the same sex or not

The second dog coming into your house should always be of the opposite sex. In almost every case dogs of the same sex do not get along well together. Dogs of the same sex, puppies, adolescents, or adults, eventually have territorial issues over food, toys, or attention from members of the family. It is almost inevitable that a nasty dogfight will ensue, often more than one. This problem can get so bad that you may have to get rid of one dog, which is heartbreaking. You can avoid the problem by starting out with dogs of the opposite sex.

### *Your two kids want a dog, but you and your spouse don't. However, you want to make them happy by getting one anyway*

This is not necessarily a wise choice. You want to make your kids happy by getting a dog and aren't sure what to do. We say don't do it. It is a mistake to get a dog for the children when the parents are not ready for the work that is involved. The entire responsibility for raising the dog always falls to the parents. Children promise on a stack of bibles that they will do all the work if they can only have a dog. They can be quite persuasive. What invariably happens, though, is that they either lose interest once the novelty wears off, get bogged down with their school and other obligations, or become absorbed with the dynamics of their social lives. It happens time and time again: the parents have to take care of the dog and end up resenting it. For the sake of your dog you too must want him and be willing to assume full responsibility for his needs, of which there are plenty.

# Nine

# *Children and Dogs*

**D**ogs and children are magic partly because their relationships seem to last forever in the hearts and minds of those involved. The memories and the feelings are treasures for a lifetime. To miss the experience is to miss a huge part of growing up. A kid bites his dog's tail and the dog knocks the kid down. They may both end up wailing, but that is really between the two of them. Dogs and children seek each other out and quickly become good friends as long as circumstances allow it. But parents may need some encouragement and some information to make this wonderful meeting a reality. Parents need to understand something about dogs as well as children in order to help create the beginning of a beautiful friendship. Here are some solutions for some of the important issues that arise when you bring the two together.

### *You plan to get a puppy soon for your two children, ages nine and eleven, and you wonder if they will relate to the new dog as a member of the family*

Some children think of their pets as younger siblings. It is best not to interfere with that, unless the dog is in danger of being abused. Usually, when a child considers a new puppy in the house to be like a brother or sister, it is a good situation. Some children regard their pet as a new friend. The wonderful thing about a dog is that he will accept any kind of relationship you want provided it is based on kindness and love.

### *Your dog bites when your children pull on his tail or grab him too hard*

Every dog has a different level of tolerance for physical discomfort and pain. You must give him a physical sensitivity test to determine his pain tolerance. Babies, toddlers, and rambunctious children have a tendency to pull on their dogs or even sit on them in an attempt to ride them like horses. Where one dog will tolerate the roughhouse play of a child, another will turn around and bite the child. Performing a physical sensitivity test will indicate how sensitive you must be when handling your dog in everyday activities and in training so that no one gets bitten. You must teach your children to handle your dog with love, praise, and affection!

### PHYSICAL SENSITIVITY TEST

There are three parts to the test: 1. the tail; 2. the toes; and 3. the skin on the rump. Test in a quiet area, with no one else present. Use caution if your dog is more than ten months old because he may bite.

#### Part one: the tail

Hold the dog in place with the help of the leash and collar. Grab the tail and pull it gently. If the dog simply looks at you, turns around and mouths your hand, and does not seem bothered, his tolerance level is safe. If he yelps, howls, or growls, his tolerance is low and he will not do well with children.

#### Part two: the toes

Use a leash and collar to hold the dog in place. Using your finger and thumb, press lightly between the dog's toes, expanding them outward. Gradually increase the pressure for several seconds until the dog shows signs of discomfort. If the dog tolerates strong pressure for ten seconds or more, looks at you, or licks you, his tolerance is high and is quite safe. If he cries, yells, tries to bite your hand, or growls, he has low tolerance and is not going to be good with children.

#### Part three: the skin on the rump

Use a leash and collar to hold the dog in place. With your left hand pull the dog's skin near the rump. Pull gently at first and then increase the pressure. When you pull the skin—from soft to medium to hard—and the dog looks at you playfully, turns around, and tries to mouth your hand, his tolerance is high and makes him safe with children. If he growls and then tries to bite you without warning, or only growls, he has no tolerance for this and could be dangerous with children.

### You are expecting a new baby and you need to know if your dog will be jealous when he is no longer an "only child"

If there is a new baby in the house, some dogs feel replaced, neglected, or moved from their order of rank. In addition, the new sounds, smells, and re-arrangement of the household may upset them. Rarely does a dog behave in a dangerous manner when a new member of the family arrives. However, just to be on the safe side, it is always best to supervise all contact between a baby and a dog and never leave them alone together. Reassure your pet with added attention and affection. This should be done at a time when the dog's competition is not around. It's not really jealousy; it has to do with territory and social rank inherent in pack order. Jealousy is a human trait.

### Even though your dog was raised around children, there is no way to know in advance whether he will accept visiting grandchildren

It is a mistake to assume that a dog is going to behave himself with an unfamiliar child. Even though he is good with children in his own family, he may or may not regard the visiting child in the same way. A dog does not regard visitors as members of his pack. He may not tolerate from a visitor what he does from his own family member with whom a bond has been established. The main factors are the dog's age, personality, and level of aggression. Close, cautious supervision is one option; another is to put the dog away to be on the safe side.

### *Your dog likes to sleep on the bed with your child*

Generally this is not a good idea. Some children are allergic to dog hair, which can cause breathing problems. Breathing in dog hair in your sleep could contribute to the development of an allergy. Cleanliness is another factor to consider. If your dog is carrying fleas, ticks, or lice, he will transfer them to the bed. Territory aggression can occur as well. By allowing your dog to sleep on the bed, he begins to claim the bed as part of his territory. Some dogs will defend it aggressively. Also, a dog that is allowed to sleep in a bed expands the behavior to all the furniture in your home. Dogs that sleep in the bed often sleep on the couch or living room chairs. It is best for the dog to have a bed of his own, which should be placed in a cozy corner of the kitchen or living room. Or it can be placed in the child's room so they can be close

### *You want to adopt an adult dog from a rescue shelter, but you live with young children*

Before adopting an adult dog it is very important to find out as much as possible about his past life, especially if you have children. Was he raised with children? Was he raised indoors? Was he socialized? Is there a history of aggressive behavior and what form did it take? Has he ever bitten anyone? These are just a few of the questions that need to be asked. A dog with an unknown past may bite over his food or possessions. The dog you bring home may have been living on the street. Such dogs must compete with other dogs for their meals. An adopted dog can be a wonderful pet. But if you do not know anything about the dog it can lead to disaster for a child. Before you bring the dog home see how he is with a child and ask all of these important questions.

### *Your children are anxious to see and play with the new litter of puppies*

Never allow children to go near a new litter of puppies by themselves. This will upset the puppies' mother. Parents can avoid biting incidents from the mother dog by supervising visitations to the newborns. No one should handle the puppies, certainly not the children, unless it is done with the utmost tact and awareness of the mother's apprehension about letting one go. Children must behave in a subdued manner around the newborns and not give the mother any cause for alarm.

### *You want to teach your children to be responsible pet owners*

When parents educate their children about dog care and dog needs they are automatically teaching the fundamentals of human principles as well. Children should be taught to view the situation from the dog's perspective. Would they like to have their tails pulled and twisted, and so on?

Each person will bond with the dog differently, and it should definitely be a family affair. Each child in the family can have a separate role in raising the dog, such as feeding, walking, training, and playing.

Involving children with such responsibilities creates a bond of friendship that makes it more difficult for children to hurt their dogs willfully. Even toddlers can help care for the family pet. This attitude, in turn, makes for a happier, more contented animal who is less likely to snap, nip, or bite. Your children will copy what you do as parents. Be gentle, sensitive, loving, and caring, and they will be, too.

## The safety of having a protection-trained dog around children

If your dog has been *professionally* trained for protection work, he will be a wonderful pet to have around children. Professionally trained dogs are very social, friendly, and loving. They make wonderful companions for every member of the family. Only the bad guys have to worry about him.

# Ten

# *The Dog Indoors*

**Y**our dog lives with a desire to be part of your family. Living indoors makes that possible. An indoor dog is usually happier and more responsive to human beings.

### *You're trying to decide if you should get a dog even though you live in an apartment*

Dogs do not care whether they live in an apartment or a large house. All they are concerned about is if you love them and how well you take care of them. Most dogs sleep a good portion of the day and it doesn't matter to them where they do this. The advantage of living in an apartment is that you will probably spend more quality time with your dog than if he were in a yard all day.

## You've just brought a dog into your apartment. What problems should you expect?

Housebreaking, excessive barking, and chewing are the most common problems, although there are others. Of course any and all of these problems can be found among dogs living anywhere. The solutions for all of these problems lie in having your dog obedience trained and by giving him an adequate amount of daily exercise.

## You need to know how to live successfully with an indoor dog in an apartment or a house

We cannot stress enough the importance of obedience training and adequate exercise for apartment dogs for their physical and mental health. You must also be able to come home during the day for a puppy and tend to his needs. If you cannot come home in the middle of the day, get a pet sitter or dog walker to come in and walk the dog, freshen his water bowl, and tend to his feeding schedule. If you have a puppy, the first year or two of his life requires a great deal of time and involvement for his well being. Young dogs and puppies need looking after several times a day. They should not be left alone for the entire day. Of course, as they mature they can stay by themselves for longer periods of time.

### *You're not sure if you should have a big dog in an apartment*

It is just fine. When it comes to apartment life, what matters most is not size, but personality. Some large dogs are couch potatoes and some small dogs are Energizer bunnies. Don't let the dog's size fool you. Obedience training is very important for an apartment dog. A well-trained dog is a happy dog and can live anywhere.

### *You want your dog to use litter boxes in the house as a toilet*

This is not recommended. It never works, at least on a consistent basis. There may be isolated cases of small dogs using a litter box inside the house, but it is not a reliable way to get your dog to relieve himself. Litter boxes should be left to cats. Dogs need to be housebroken and then walked or allowed outside to do their duty. Besides, a nice walk several times a day helps a dog get some exercise, relieve his boredom, enjoy sensory stimulation, and become much more socialized and adaptive to new people, new dogs, and new situations.

### *You want to use a crate for your dog and are wondering what is the proper size to buy*

The dog crate is a wonderful way to confine your dog indoors when it becomes necessary. The only crates acceptable for this purpose are those made of thin wire bars so the dog can look out from all sides as he enjoys good ventilation. The floor of the crate should be made of a smooth solid material such as Masonite or metal, and it must have a hinged door large enough for the dog to walk through. The size of the crate is correct if your dog can stand up in it and turn around comfortably. Small dogs should not be housed in crates that are obviously too large for them. Dogs have an instinct to create a small, cozy den in which to sleep and rest and enjoy their privacy. This is exactly what wolves and wild dogs do. Because of this den instinct dogs need to be left alone in a confined space at certain times. You will find that eventually you will be able to leave the door to the crate open at all times so that your dog can go in and rest at his own discretion. The crate is a wonderful tool with which to confine your dog during housebreaking. It is also useful for preventing destructive behavior. The crate can also keep your dog out of trouble when you have a large party or houseguests staying overnight.

### You want to know if it is necessary to get your dog his own special bed

It is not necessary at all, but many pet owners enjoy giving the family dog a comfortable or plush bed of his own. Lots of dogs like having their own beds and seem to luxuriate in them. Occasionally a dog fancies sleeping on a big fluffy pillow. You can't help but smile at a small dog who runs to his pillow, leaps into the center of it, and pushes in a shallow nest in which to curl up. Of course there are many dogs that want no part of a bed and prefer to sleep on the floor or on the carpet. Go figure.

### *Your dog seems to need more exercise if he is kept indoors most of the time*

This is true. You must set aside time for your dog to exercise. Creating a schedule for this and sticking to it is the best thing you can do for him. Bear in mind that there is a very fine line between exercise and play. Exercise does not only consist of long walks and runs but also retrieving games with the use of a ball or a Frisbee. The point is that exercising your dog can and should be fun for both of you. It is one of the best ways for you to bond with him as you both get into shape. Who knows, you may end up doing a marathon together.

### *You are considering getting an adult dog for your apartment*

The first and foremost advantage is avoiding the work and inconveniences of the puppy phase of a dog's life, made more inconvenient in an apartment. Adult dogs do not have the inevitable problems of puppies and as a result make the adjustment to a new home easier and quicker. Dogs that are one year of age or older are easier to train and take less time to do it because of their maturity. However, it is important to take into consideration the previous history and lifestyle of a mature dog. Be certain that he has had some experience as an indoor dog. A puppy presents many enjoyable and lovable adventures as he grows and develops from one phase to another. He also presents sleepless nights as he cries for his mother, his litter mates, and his previous home. He gets into everything and can be a danger to himself as he bites into electric cords, knocks over lamps, pees all over the floor, and chews on books, records, and shoes. An older dog has already finished with most of this nerve-wracking behavior and is a lot more adaptive to apartment life as soon as you bring him home.

### You believe it is cruel to have a dog in an apartment

It is not cruel at all. This is a myth. Virtually hundreds of thousands of dogs live in city apartments, and what is the alternative? Not a pleasant thought. Dogs that live in apartments often get more attention than dogs that stay in a yard all day. Obedience training at an early age is essential if your dog lives in an apartment because of the close living quarters. Apartment dogs should get a midday walk. If you are unable to come home during the day, consider a pet sitter or dog walker who could be a friend, relative, or neighbor. A dog doesn't know the difference between an apartment and a house; he just knows that you love him and he loves living with you. Where is the cruelty in that? It is true that some breeds need more exercise than others do, so this should be taken into consideration when selecting a dog in the first place.

*Eleven*

# The Dog Outdoors

*I*t is obvious that puppies and very young dogs should not be left outdoors all night. It is just too cold and unsocializing. However, if you insist that your pet be an outdoor dog then you must provide him with a warm, comfortable doghouse in a secure environment where he cannot wander off to roam. The outdoor dog is vulnerable to all kinds of trouble, such as dognapping, poisoning, dogfights, digging behavior, and more.

### You let your dog sleep outside all the time

We prefer allowing a dog to be inside the home, at least part of the time. Living outdoors twenty-four hours a day in our view is not the best thing. A dog is a member of the family. If he stays outside all day and all night he has no opportunity to be socialized properly to people. This can lead to the development of shy or aggressive behavior later in the dog's life. There is no reason why a dog should have to stay outside all of the time. With proper training, he can be a well-behaved, enjoyable member of the family. Why would you have any member of your family sleep outside all the time?

### You have been trying to get an adopted dog that was raised outside adjusted to living indoors as well

Begin with three or four days of bonding techniques before leaving him alone. Bonding involves developing an emotional connection with the dog by being very affectionate, increasing close contact, talking to him, giving him food treats, and taking advantage of any other opportunity that creates closeness. See Chapter 2, "How to Get Your Dog to Love You." Start by placing the dog in a small area indoors, such as the kitchen. Keep expanding the size of the area after he is secure in the one you started with. This will take some time, so be patient. Obedience training and daily exercise are essential in order to prevent chewing and other destructive behaviors. Keep the dog confined to the one area of your house until you are certain that he is fully adjusted to being indoors.

### You want to keep your dog outdoors most of the time. What problems should you expect?

- *digging,* which can make your lawn look like craters on the moon

- *excessive barking.* (Your neighbors will learn to hate you.)
- *jumping over fences,* which represents a threat to the dog's safety and the comfort of your community. Remember, not everyone appreciates an unrestricted dog approaching him or her. An unrestricted dog is one way to lose good relations with your neighbors.

### You leave food outside all day for your outdoor dog

We do not recommend leaving food out for several reasons. First, most food tends to spoil. Second, it is an invitation for creatures in the neighborhood to take your dog's dinner. Third, there is always the possibility that your dog will either be overfed or underfed. Make other arrangements. Use a pet sitter to visit and feed the dog at a sensible time. Another option is the use of an automatic feeder. These are clever utensils readily available at pet supply stores and in catalogs. Remember to have plenty of water available at all times.

### You need to prevent your dog from developing heat stroke in the summer, especially if you live in a hot climate

Make sure that your dog has access to an area that is covered and provides a cool, shaded area, even if it is outside. If you are not at home, a doggie door is very useful. Your dog will love you for it. A child's plastic wading pool filled with cool water is helpful. Your dog can splash around in the water to stay cool and enjoy himself at the same time. Make sure there is plenty of fresh drinking water available. Some dogs will tip their water bowl, which can be a problem in the summer when the weather is hot and he needs to be able to drink all day. There are several devices available that attach to an outside water faucet making water accessible to the dog at all times. It is very simple to teach your dog to use this, and they will love you for it. Another alternative is to provide access to the indoors, where fresh water is always available.

### Your dog jumps in your pool

Prevention is the most important thing. Start by obedience training your dog as soon as possible at a young age. Teach the command "place." This will allow you to command your dog to go to a specific area and stay until you give him a command that releases him. If your dog is trained he will certainly respond to the command "no," which is invaluable. Just saying "no" without training has little or no effect. But when "no" has been taught as a training command with the techniques provided in Chapter 3 it becomes highly effective. Providing an outdoor dog run is another effective way to prevent his jumping into the pool. This enables the dog to have freedom to move around while in a safe, controlled environment.

### You let your dog swim in your pool

Most dogs can swim, but some are too frightened to do it or smart enough to see the limitations of the situation. Never make the assumption that your dog can swim until you try him out in a safe, controlled environment. Make sure the swimming area has an easy way for the dog to enter and exit the water on his own. A dog must be able to scramble out of the water when necessary, and that requires a swimming area with a tapered bottom beneath the water. The beaches at the ocean and at some lakes provide this, as do many swimming pools.

### *You want to take your dog to the beach*

The ocean surf, strong undertows, and cross currents are just as dangerous for dogs as for humans. A dog in water over his head struggling with the surf is just as likely to panic as anyone else and may require being rescued. Stay alert and watch your dog as you would a child when he is in the water. You just may have to save him from drowning. Play in water that is not deep and call him back if he starts to go too far out. When calling him back, try to sound upbeat so that he'll want to come back, as though it were a game.

### *You have both grass and a cement patio in your yard, but you don't know which is best for your dog*

For sanitary conditions, cement is the best surface because it is easier to clean and gives less opportunity for disease to thrive. A cement surface also strengthens your dog's foot pads by toughening up the tissue. Grass is soft and easy for a dog to dig into, but do you really want a dug-up lawn? And what about yellow grass?

### You're not sure about the right size for a fence that properly confines your dog in the backyard

A backyard fence should be at least six feet high. To be on the safe side, eight feet is even better. Some dogs are capable of climbing over very high fences. If you have such a dog you should consider building a fence that has a solid surface made of wood or cinder block rather than one made of chain link. Keep the area near the fence clear of any items that the dog can use as a boost up to help him jump over. Many dogs are great escape artists.

The best solution is to have a dog run built or to purchase a portable dog run. This will ensure that the dog is properly confined and cannot leave the yard. It will probably save his life.

### Your spouse argues that your dog belongs outside the house

The conflict is based on you wanting the dog to be part of the family and live inside as well as outside. This is a common conflict in many households with a dog. Raising a dog can present many issues that were not anticipated. In some cases it is a cultural issue, where one member of the family is used to having animals that were used for working and cannot imagine them as part of the family. This is a large issue that is difficult to work out after the dog is brought home. It must be discussed and settled *before* getting a family dog. If both parties are willing to compromise, then the dog could be outside during the day and inside during the night. It can only be settled by both parties being willing to change to some degree.

### You're worried about diseases that can be acquired by dogs and transmitted to humans

If your dog spends most of his time outdoors, he is more at risk for disease. Diseases that can be transmitted from animals to humans are called zoonoses. Although there are approximately 150 viral, bacterial, and fungal zoonoses, only a few can be transmitted from dogs, cats, and other pets to humans. However, those few can be serious and dog owners must be aware of them. The most serious is rabies, a disease borne from a virus. A human (or a dog) bitten by an animal infected with rabies will almost certainly be infected with this life-threatening disease. A number of bacteria-induced illnesses can also be passed from dog to human, most of which come from dog bites, but can also be transmitted from close contact without washing hands, such as salmonellosis. Some bacteria are transmitted by parasites such as ticks, fleas, and various forms of worms. The most common form of fungus-induced zoonotic disease is ringworm. If your dog is outdoors most of the time, make sure he is properly vaccinated, sees a veterinarian regularly, and lives in a hygienic environment. This requires that you become knowledgeable about your dog's medical needs. Have a serious talk with your veterinarian on this subject and indicate your concern. Purchase a quality book on the subject of medical care for dogs and use it. See the Recommended Reading section at the end of this book.

## Your dog's personality seems affected by living outdoors all the time

When your dog is left outside all of the time, he has little opportunity to socialize with people other than those who care for him. If your dog never gets to meet other dogs he may become shy or aggressive from fear of strangers or noises. As such a dog matures, he may also become too territorial. Lack of socialization is one of the major causes of dog aggression toward people and other dogs.

## You want to install a doggie door

What a wonderful invention! The doggie door provides the best of both worlds. It is simply a small door on a two-way hinge attached to an appropriate opening created through the wall of your home and leading to the outside. It allows your dog to come and go as he pleases. It is a great tool for housebreaking because the dog always has access to the inside or outside of the house no matter what the weather may be. It also allows the owner more freedom because it eliminates the need for a walking schedule. The dog is able to get the exercise that he wants and needs on his own. A doggie door can be purchased at many hardware and houseware stores, pet supply stores, and through catalogs, or can be custom-built by a carpenter.

## Your dog barks all the time when he is outside

The first thing to do is investigate. Try to determine the reason that the dog is barking and eliminate the cause, if possible. The most important part of the solution is obedience training for your dog. Before you can do anything you must be able to control him so that he obeys you. See the section on barking in Chapter 20, "He's Driving Me Crazy."

### *Your outdoor dog digs holes in the yard*

There are many reasons why dogs dig. The most important reason for digging is the instinct to create a den for himself. In his natural state the wild dog (and the wolf) either finds a cave or creates something like one in order to curl up in it and feel safe when resting and sleeping. It's like making a bed. (See the section on digging in Chapter 20.) Dogs do not dig holes as a way of expressing anger at you. They do not do anything out of spite or anger. These are human behaviors. It is one of the important reasons we love them as we do. Keeping your dog indoors more allows less opportunity for digging.

# Twelve

# *Getting Along with Other Animals*

**Y** *our* dog may have to share his world with another pet, presenting the inexperienced owner with a number of concerns that may or may not lead to problems such as competition for attention, a struggle for dominance, fighting, or simply the question of who gets to eat first. These are some of the issues when a dog lives in a natural state with a pack. These are the elements that create pack harmony. All dogs are social creatures owing to inherited instincts that are drawn from pack behavior. The dog (or wolf) pack is essentially a small family living together in a very specific social organization. If your dog is left alone much of the time, as many pet dogs are, he is living out an existence similar to that of the lone wolf. It is not what nature intended. For many, the answer lies in the pleasure of living with two, or even more, dogs. For others the answer is to keep a dog and a cat. If your dog lives with another dog or even a cat problems can arise, and following are some solutions.

### The benefits of getting a second dog

There are two obvious benefits, for both dogs and people. If you have one great dog in your life, why not have two? The more the merrier. You will get twice as much of whatever pleasure you get from the one dog. For most people it is about love. The dogs get another form of companionship from each other. They will probably play with each other so that you won't have to exercise them very much. What you must consider about having more than one dog, however, is the added expense. They will cost you twice as much for food, veterinary care, boarding when you go away, leashes, collars, and all the rest. With one dog you may be able to get away without dog training, but two dogs make obedience training an absolute necessity.

### Getting two dogs at the same time

This is not a good idea. The two dogs are most likely going to bond with each other exclusively and become somewhat detached from the human family. Another reason not to get them at the same time is for the sake of evaluation. It is hard for a family to evaluate either of the dogs' personalities when they are always together. Knowing your dog's personality is important for dog training and individual attention. It's like trying to understand twins. You cannot give each dog personalized attention when they are bonded together because they will never be apart if they can help it. Some dogs socialize with each other rather than with people. Of course they will love their families but may not necessarily be very social with humans outside of their family. The ideal situation is to wait six months to a year before getting a second dog. It will certainly be less work for you, because you won't have the needs of two dogs to contend with at the same time. A new dog must be housebroken, taught not to chew, trained, played with, and much more. Doing all these things for two puppies at the same time is a lot of work. Are you ready for that?

### Getting two males, two females, or two dogs of the opposite sex

When you choose to live with two dogs it is best that they each be of the opposite sex. Dogs of opposite gender have very little or no aggression toward each other, and they are more likely to get along. Dogs of the same sex, whether males or females, are more likely to fight with each other as they reach sexual maturity. This begins to take place after one year. Same-sex problems depend on the personality of each dog. If they both have dominant personalities the aggression will be intense between them. If one is subordinate to the other there is a chance that they will get along.

### Getting a second dog as a way of solving the behavior problems of the first dog

This is not a valid reason for getting a second dog. It will not work. A second dog will not solve the behavior problems of the first. As a matter of fact, he may create additional problems, such as the more serious consequences of dogfighting. If your dog has a behavior problem it must be solved on a one-to-one basis. See Chapter 20, "He's Driving Me Crazy."

### *Bringing a puppy into a house where there is already an older dog*

This is a great idea for many reasons. It will compel the older dog to be more playful and give him more exercise than he would get otherwise. The puppy should be of the opposite sex so that they will get along once the newcomer grows up. Either way, the older dog is going to have a new boyfriend or girlfriend. We know a German Shepherd Dog named Ullie who is nine years old and is now living with a young female Corgi named Pebbles. She is driving him crazy in a wonderful way. All they do is play. He is so much happier and has even lost some of his excess weight. It is a win-win situation.

### *The proper way to introduce a new dog to one already living with you*

Always introduce the dogs on neutral territory. For example, go to a park or some place away from the house. Even down the street, not too close to your residence, will do. Dogs are very territorial. It is a mistake to introduce them in your home, where they are both going to live. There may be serious dog aggression in the initial contact if one dog decides to defend his territory. When you take them to the meeting place make sure both dogs are on a leash. Allow them to sniff each other. They will get along eventually, especially if they are of the opposite sex. It should be no problem. New dogs of the same sex are the ones that are likely to have aggression problems.

### Dogs that are aggressive at home but not in the park

Most dogs are territorial about where they live, whether they are in their house or yard. There is a strong need in many dogs to defend their turf from other dogs and strangers. Defending territory is not an issue at the park because it is neutral ground. Aggression between dogs that are away from home is usually about issues of dominance.

### Dogs and cats living together

Dogs and cats are not natural enemies. One of the secrets of enabling them to live together is to bring in a kitten to live with an older dog, or have an older cat and bring in a puppy. It is a matter of socializing them together, allowing them to play with each other and allowing one or the other to be the dominant animal. Nevertheless, do not allow an older dog to chase or bully a kitten. In that situation place your dog in a down/stay position and allow the kitten to get used to him. Another way to introduce them safely is to place the kitten in a crate and let the dog sniff around and get used to him without being able to harass the kitten in any way. This will work for a puppy with an older cat too. The problems between a cat and a dog are often territorial in nature. Sometimes the chase instinct is triggered in the dog when a cat runs past, causing the dog to chase.

### *The best way to have your dog around other animals, whether walking down the street or going to the vet*

It is very important to maintain control of your dog in these situations, and there is no better way than to have him obedience trained. One of the most useful commands is down/stay. This command not only brings the dog under control, but also puts him automatically in a subordinate position. Once he is down he will not behave as aggressively as he would if he were standing and in a dominant position. The more your dog is socialized with other animals, whether walking down the street, in the park, or at a training class, the more at ease he will become with members of his extended family.

### *Why some dogs are more aggressive or shy with some dogs and not with others*

The most probable reason for this is lack of socialization. Aggressiveness or shyness with other dogs is common in dogs that are kept in the backyard and rarely if ever allowed to be with other animals. As they get older, they get more territorial, more aggressive, or more fearful, which causes shyness. That is why it is so important to socialize your dog at a young age. Another possible reason for this behavior might be a frightening experience, such as being attacked by an-

other dog as a puppy. That would cause him to become fearful and aggressive. A solution for this is to
obedience train your dog and work him around other
dogs. As you do this, do not allow him to behave in an
aggressive way. Once your dog is obedient he will not
act aggressively if you correct him every time he does.

## Thirteen

# *Playing Around*
## (Toys)

**P***lay* is one of the most important learning activities for all dogs, including puppies, adolescents, and seniors. Play offers the opportunity for a dog or a puppy to learn and practice survival behavior without consequences. When dogs wrestle or pounce on one another, as they do when they play, they are actually practicing what to do in the event of a real fight or when hunting. Play behavior is a rehearsal of fighting for territory, escape techniques, establishing social rank, and various aspects of capturing a prey animal for food. Nature never anticipated domestication and the pet industry's prolific marketing of dog toys that are designed to appeal to dogs and humans alike. Nevertheless, play is fun and play is valuable. The more you play with your dog the more he learns and, as a bonus, enjoys being with you. Your dog's desire to play is either with you, other dogs, or by himself.

### Playing with your dog

Play with your dog whenever you can, providing it does not interfere with his feeding, training, or need to rest. The nice thing is that you can exercise him and play with him at the same time by tossing toys, rolling a ball, or throwing a Frisbee. There is no such thing as having too much fun with your dog. Playing with your dog strengthens the bond with him and even benefits obedience training. Play time is also exercise time. You can have fun by watching or joining in. Exercise helps keep your dog healthy and happy. Please remember that if your dog doesn't work off his energy outside, he will work it off inside—and you know what that means! Overweight or arthritic dogs benefit greatly from the fun and the exercise. What can be better for your relationship than play?

### The proper way to play with your dog

Many dog owners do not know that there is a right way and a wrong way to play with a dog. Playing with your dog properly is very important. There is no big mystery about it. You simply play in a positive manner. You can get down on the floor to play with your friend. Roll over together and do the sorts of things you would with a baby who is old enough to crawl. Retrieving a stick or a ball is another positive way to play with your dog. It gives you the added benefit of teaching him to come to you when you call him. Make cuddling and hugging part of the play. The wrong way is to play games that encourage aggressive behavior; these represent the wrong ways to play with a dog. Do not play games that encourage pulling with his teeth, such as tug-of-war. Do not tease your dog for fun and do not allow him to jump on you just for the fun of it. This encourages aggressiveness and contradicts obedience training.

### Exercise for outdoor dogs

Dogs enjoy having someone to play with. When you get home, place your dog's exercise high on your list of priorities. Your dog must be exercised at least once a day for five to twenty minutes, depending on his age and personality. If you have a couch potato, you will need to exercise him more than you would a highly energetic dog.

### The best play and exercise surface for your puppy

Puppy paw pads are soft and thin-skinned. A puppy's bones are still growing and hardening. You must be careful not to damage their delicate bodies. Running around and playing on a hard surface can damage bones and skin tissue. The young dog is much better off playing on grass or dirt. You must also be careful about puppies running and playing on slippery surfaces such as tile, marble, or polished wood floors. They can lose their footing easily and slide into a wall or piece of furniture and become injured.

### Games that can teach obedience

Playing games with your dog can be educational as much as they are fun. Tossing a ball to your dog, for example, teaches two commands. Your dog learns to retrieve the ball and bring it back to you, and also to release the ball on your command. Remember that playing should be fun for the both of you.

### Swimming for play and exercise

Most dogs instinctively know how to swim. Some do not. Bulldogs, for instance, cannot swim because of their body type; their short legs and hefty body make swimming very difficult. They sink like a rock. There are devices such as life jackets that are wonderful to use if you want the dog in the water with you. Flotation apparatus is essential if you go boating with a dog, especially if you sail far from the shore.

### How to tell the difference between dogs playing with each other and dogs beginning a dogfight

Fights usually start shortly after two dogs are introduced to each other. When two dominant dogs meet, particularly if they are of the same sex, they will try to challenge each other. You may see them raise their hackles, project their chests, raise their heads, elevate their tails high above their rumps, and lock eyes on each other. If neither dog backs down, a fight is almost sure to start; they will attempt to determine which is the most dominant dog. When dogs play together, they pretend to bite, growl, and generally roughhouse with each other. It can build in pitch and intensity, but it rarely turns into a fight unless they are of the same sex. Dogs of opposite sex rarely fight each other, but it can happen.

### Dogs that nip while playing

Nipping is never acceptable behavior. If your dog nips you with his teeth he must be corrected, no matter if it is a full bite or a half-bite on your arm or a bit of a nibble on your fingers or ankles. Teething in puppies and young dogs often causes nipping behavior. Even so, you must correct this whenever and wherever it happens. Please refer to Chapter 20, "He's Driving Me Crazy." Dogs should never be allowed to nip you because it is teaching him that it's okay to bite.

### Dogs that do not like to play

The personality of a dog determines whether he enjoys play or not. Some dogs are all business and are too serious-minded for play. Some like chew toys, some like only balls, and then again, some dogs are uninterested in playing with any kind of toys. If you have a dog that doesn't like to play, you need to be innovative. Try exercise as a way of lightening him up and putting him in some kind of a playing frame of mind. Try running, retrieving, playing with other dogs, agility classes, obedience trials, or any form of activity that sparks your dog's interest. Play and exercise are good for the body and very good for the mind.

# Fourteen

# Groom with a View

**W**hen your dog walks into the room and everyone else leaves, it's time to think about the "g" word. No dog should smell like an elephant or look like the unswept floor of a barbershop. Every dog, even a fuzzball as big as a Volkswagen, has a bit of elegance and a touch of class just waiting to shine through with a dip in the tub and a gentle plow with a comb and brush. We're talking about dog grooming, which at its best is a highly skilled occupation when practiced by a trained professional and almost always results in a beautiful-looking dog. If you consider the hundreds of dog breeds, each with their own grooming requirements, you begin to understand how demanding it is to be a professional dog groomer. The typical dog owner, however, should not be as concerned with grooming for breed standards as set forth by the American Kennel Club or the United Kennel Club but for the sake of hygiene and health. Of course, everyone wants their dog to look nice, and good grooming practices accomplish that, but as a secondary consideration. For those who wish to spend the money, dog-grooming salons are easily found in the phone book just about everywhere. This chapter, however, is mostly concerned with basic grooming for the sake of cleanliness, good health, and a reasonably attractive appearance.

### Bathing your dog

*How often you should bathe your dog.* It depends on the breed, coat length and texture, coat color, whether the dog lives indoors or outdoors, and the cleanliness of his environment. Obviously, a white or light-colored dog will look dirty much sooner than one with a dark coat. A dog with a long coat has more hair to show dirt, and of course mats and tangles are always a problem. An indoor dog living in a clean house does not get as dirty as one that lives outdoors or in a messy house. Frequent baths are not usually necessary. Dogs competing in dog shows are bathed as much as once a week when they are being campaigned, but with the proper shampoo and bathing techniques suffer no harm to their skin or coat. Frequent baths are not advised for dogs with double coats such as the Akita, Alaskan Malamute, Chow Chow, Rough Collie, German Shepherd Dog, Keeshond, Samoyed, Shetland Sheepdog, Siberian Husky, and other similar dogs. Too many baths tends to soften their rough outer or top coat, depleting its weather-resistance quality. It is not excessive, however, to bathe any dog once every two months or whenever he is dirty and smells bad. A bath not only cleans the skin and coat, but also has the important benefits of removing harmful bacteria as well as external parasites and their droppings. Almost every dog will tolerate a bath, and some even like it.

#### WHAT YOU WILL NEED

- Shampoo formulated specifically for dogs. Among the dog shampoos available are: tearless; for sensitive skin and for various coat colors; medicated (for skin problems); for flea and tick removal; and even waterless ones that are rubbed in and brushed out.
- crème rinse to remove shampoo residue and soften the hair
- coat conditioner and coat dressing for good looks and easier brushing
- a tub mat to prevent the dog from slipping
- shampoo brush
- Vaseline or mineral oil to prevent soap from getting in the eyes
- cotton balls to prevent water from splashing in the ears
- washcloth
- two large towels
- portable spray hose that attaches to a faucet or a

garden hose for outdoor baths
- an electric hair dryer (optional)

*What to do just before the bath.* Do not bathe a dog that has matted or tangled hair. You must first brush them out and untangle them. If you do not, the mats and tangles will tighten and become much harder to undo. The two worst things that can happen during a bath are to get soap in the dog's eyes or to get water in his ears. Both events are painful and very stressful. To avoid this, place a wad of absorbent cotton in each of the dog's ears so that water cannot get down into the canals. Set them in firmly but do not allow them to travel too far down. Next, take an eyedropper and squirt a drop or two of mineral oil in the dog's eyes to protect them against the burning sensation of shampoo. A pinch of Vaseline will do the same job when smeared in the corners of each eye. Place a thin film of Vaseline on the dog's genitalia and around the anus to avoid shampoo irritation. Place a bath mat on the tub surface. It is not good for a dog to be standing belly-high in water. Fill the tub with no more than two inches of warm water and a small quantity of shampoo so that standing in it will automatically clean the paws. This will also soften the paw pads and clean between the toes with little effort.

### Washing the dog

Thoroughly wet the dog's entire body with luke-warm water. You can use a spray hose or a plastic container filled with water. A spray hose makes the job easier and quicker. He may try to run or jump once the water is applied, so spray his feet first to avoid panic and talk to him in a soothing, reassuring tone of voice. Once the paws are wet, soak the legs. Spraying against the fur, soak the sides of the torso and under the ribs and stomach. Spray the tail and backside. Be gentle. Wet the top of the body (against the fur) starting from back to front to avoid scaring him. Never use your spray on the dog's head or face. Wet the head, face, and ears last using a dripping washcloth.

Use the shampoo according to the manufacturer's instructions. If the dog has fleas, apply the shampoo from the front to the back to prevent them from scurrying to the ears and other hiding places. Lather the shampoo with your fingers and push it through the fur vigorously so that it reaches down to the skin.

Work the suds along the spine from the neck to the tail and then around the entire torso. Lather the tail, the anus, the hindquarters, and the genitals. Working downward, lather each leg to the paws. Clean them by spreading each toe and lathering inside. These are hiding places for ticks and fleas. Do not lather the dog's head until last, taking care to avoid soap in the eyes and ears.

Next, scrub the dog's entire body with a shampoo brush so that old dander and debris is washed away with any dead ticks or fleas.

You may now rinse the soap thoroughly with the spray. Thick, coarse coats may require shampooing the dog twice. Drain the tub before the final rinse. Remove every trace of shampoo in the last rinse and continue to spray the dog until the water from the body runs clear. At this stage follow the manufacturer's instructions for the crème rinse, hair conditioner, or flea and tick dip if you choose to use any of these products.

Squeeze and press the water from the coat with your hands. Remove the dog from the tub and allow him to give himself a good shake or two. Cover him with a towel and blot the water off instead of rubbing it away as most humans do after a bath.

In warm weather a short-hair dog may simply dry outdoors with a brushing afterward. Long-hair dogs and dogs living in apartments should be dried with a handheld electric hair dryer. Place the dog on a dry towel for warmth and absorbency. Switch the setting to "warm" rather than "hot." Start drying with the top of the head. Do not point the dryer directly into the face. Dry the torso first, then the legs, and finally the tail.

A long-hair coat will dry to a silky, fluffy texture if you brush the coat as you blow-dry it. Brush with the nap of the fur in light, upward strokes as you blow warm air in the same direction. Do this in layers for quicker drying time. For the areas that have dried too soon or become unmanageable, spray a bit of water or coat conditioner on them. That completes the bath.

### Daily brushing and combing

A daily grooming effort is necessary to maintain good hygiene and good looks. It also avoids the difficulty of having to deal with mats and tangles in the medium- to long-coated dogs. The hair coat is the outer beauty of any dog, and by brushing and combing it on a regular basis you can maintain it with ease and very little effort. A dog that is brushed regularly does not need frequent baths. Dirt on a dog's body that is not brushed away can cause a variety of skin ailments that range from annoying to very serious. Bear in mind that whatever is in or on a dog's body eventually will get into the human living areas where he spends each day and night. Some dogs lick themselves and swallow all manner of harmful debris, from parasites to broken glass. Daily brushing and combing removes dead hair and removes or prevents minor mats and tangles. It also smoothes out the coat, giving it a pleasing appearance. The skin beneath the fur should be inspected when being groomed and checked for lumps, cuts, or skin lesions. Daily combing and brushing, which takes no more than five minutes, also keeps shedding problems manageable.

## Getting the right brush

### BRISTLE BRUSH

This is the one grooming tool needed by all dog owners for the care of long-, medium-, and short-coated dogs. Bristle brushes are available with all-nylon bristles, a combination of nylon and natural bristles, all-natural bristles, or all-natural bristles surrounding the center rows of nylon bristles. The brush you select should be suitable for your dog's size, coat length, and coat texture. The bristles should be tapered, with some long enough to penetrate through the coat down to the skin. Nylon bristle brushes are not recommended for every dog breed because of their hardness and stiffness. Consult a groomer or pet supplies dealer for the proper size and type for your dog.

### PIN BRUSH

These are used to groom long- and medium-coated dogs of both small and large breeds, such as Cocker Spaniels, Borzois, Afghans, Shih Tzus, Lhasa Apsos, or Shetland Sheepdogs. A pin brush has long or short stainless steel or chrome-plated pins with rounded ends to prevent irritating or scratching the dog's skin. The pins should be flexible and bend a bit when run through a long coat if the hair is stiff or coarse. They are always set in a soft rubber base and remain highly flexible. The pins come in short, medium, and long lengths and are selected on the basis of the length of a dog's coat.

### SLICKER BRUSH

Rectangular in shape, these have wooden handles. Short, bent-wire teeth placed closely together characterize slicker brushes. They are available in small, medium, and large sizes and are best for dogs with medium-length coats such as Poodles and several of the terrier breeds. Their purpose is to untangle mats and remove dead hair.

### RUBBER BRUSH

Made of one molded piece of rubber that includes the teeth, this brush is for grooming and polishing short- and smooth-coated breeds. The rubber brush also can be used for shampooing and massaging the skin without scratching or irritating sensitive dogs. It is of no use in grooming long- or medium-coated dogs.

### Getting the right comb

Dog combs are available in stainless steel, chrome-plated brass, and high quality aluminum. Be certain the points of the teeth are smooth and rounded, not harsh or sharp. Match the length and spacing of the teeth to your dog's coat. The long, harsh, and fluffed-out coat of a Chow Chow requires a comb with much longer teeth than the comb you would need for a Yorkshire Terrier, with its long, silky coat that is thin and lies flat. A fine-tooth comb is best for a soft, thin, or silky coat. For average coat lengths such as on German Shepherd Dogs and Golden Retrievers, professionals use medium-tooth combs. A coarse-tooth comb with widely spaced apart teeth is best on long, harsh coats or long, profuse coats like the kind found on Old English Sheepdogs.

#### HALF-MEDIUM, HALF-FINE COMB

This is a very useful comb for most breeds. The fine teeth are best for soft or silky hair; the medium teeth are used for coats of average texture. Both medium and fine teeth are used on different sections of the same dog's coat. Half-medium, half-fine combs are made of various sizes and length of teeth to accommodate almost any type of coat.

#### MATTING COMB (OR RAKE COMB)

When the fur of very heavy-coated breeds such as the Old English Sheepdog or the Newfoundland becomes tangled and matted, a matting comb is extremely useful; it helps undo the twisting and matted fur. This special style comb comes in several sizes, with or without handles.

### SHEDDING BLADE

This very useful tool is simply a thin metal blade that has been bent around in a loop and is held together with a leather handle. The blade is similar to a hacksaw blade with serrated teeth on its cutting underside. It is used for stripping away the dead hair from most coats. It is essential to use on dogs that are constant shedders to keep their coats healthy.

### *Brushing and combing*

Before brushing any dog, spray a light mist of water or coat conditioner over the coat. This will neutralize static electricity, eliminate dryness, and help to remove tangles as well as add luster to the hair. Moisturizing the coat also makes brushing and combing a smoother and easier task.

*Long-coated dogs* should be brushed daily with a pin brush and a bristle brush and then combed out to maintain the luster and prevent the fur from matting. This also keeps the coat clean and stimulates the skin. Long flowing coats should be brushed in layers, from the skin out to the ends of the hair, with the pin brush. Start with the legs and work up to the body coat in small sections at a time. When brushing the coat on the body, start at the chest and work your way to the rear, brushing downward with long, sweeping motions. Use your comb to separate the hair down the middle of the back with a part. The comb is also useful for hair that feathers away from the body on the legs, ears, neck, chest, underside of the body, and the tail. Many breeds have such "feathering"; i.e., the Irish Setter, Golden Retriever, and most spaniels.

**Double-coated dogs,** such as the German Shepherd Dog, Siberian Husky, and Welsh Corgis, have harsh topcoats, usually in short- or medium-length, and a soft, downy undercoat. Use a bristle brush in addition to a pin brush. Start at the hindquarters and work toward the head. Finish by combing out the hair, paying particular attention to mats or tangles.

**Hard- and wiry-coated dogs** such as many of the terrier breeds like the Airedale, and such as the Standard and Giant Schnauzer, should be brushed with a bristle brush. Stroke the brush in the direction that the wiry hair grows to avoid breaking off clumps of hair.

**Short- and medium-coated dogs with a smooth surface**—including the Beagle, Boxer, Doberman Pinscher, Labrador Retriever, Rottweiler, and Weimaraner among many others—should be groomed once or twice a week for good looks and to avoid excessive shedding. Massage the coat with your fingers to loosen dead and broken hair. With a medium-to-firm bristle brush, stroke the hair in the direction in which it grows. Get the brush deep down to the skin. Comb the hair out after brushing. To get a smooth, polished look complete the job by rubbing the coat with a silk handkerchief or chamois for a bright luster.

## *Coping with shedding dog hair*

Shedding is dead hair falling from your dog's coat; it clings to household surfaces and your clothing. It is the process of a dog casting off one layer of hair as it is replaced with another. Nature's purpose is to replace the heavy winter coat with a lighter one for summer. As the weather becomes colder, the reverse takes place. It is about insulation. Shedding the winter coat begins in the spring, and under normal conditions takes approximately three weeks. Shedding the summer coat and replacing it with a heavier one occurs in autumn, preparing the dog for cold weather and the time span varies from dog to dog. Some dogs shed once a year throughout a long cycle that achieves the same effect, giving the impression that such dogs shed all the time. Although all dogs cast off their coats, some breeds shed much more than others. Long-coated dogs do not shed more than short-coated dogs; because each hair is long it does accumulate in greater volume. Nothing will prevent your dog from shedding. However, there are several ways to reduce the impact. Feed your dog a well-balanced diet as found in premium commercial pet foods. Many animal experts have suggested that an occasional teaspoon of cooked animal fat such as that from bacon or beef helps to keep shedding to a minimum. Dogs that sleep near heat sources such as radiators tend to shed more because their skin and coat will be drier. Because there is a relationship between shedding and the length of seasonal daylight (longer days in the spring and summer), keeping your dog under artificial light for long periods of time may trigger the body's shedding response. Bathe your dog more frequently than usual during the shedding season. To avoid pipe clogs, place a strainer in the tub drain to catch the hair. It is also helpful to apply a commercial coat conditioner to relieve dry skin, dull coat, and shedding hair. The most important thing you can do to reduce the need for constantly cleaning up shed hair is to comb and brush your dog every day. This will rid the dog of most of the dead hair and loose dander before it falls on your carpet or your navy blue suit.

### Trimming your dog's nails

Unclipped nails that are allowed to grow beyond the point where they touch the surface of the ground can throw a dog off balance and become a hazard. Extra-long nails sometimes curl under the pads and become painful as the dog tries to walk or run. However, if a dog is walked frequently on a concrete or asphalt surface, it will help keep them worn down. Nails are either light or dark in color. Light nails are easier to trim because you can see where the transparent area ends and the nerve endings in the quick of the nail begins. Clipping beyond the transparent area is painful to the dog and will cause bleeding. This is especially a risk when the nails are dark-colored. Have your vet show you the proper place to clip. A good rule to follow is to cut at the point where the nails begin to curve. The bottom of the nail should be even with the bottom of the pad. It is safer to cut too little than too much. Trimming your dog's nails is an important but often neglected chore. It requires a special tool. You will need a set of nail trimmers designed specifically for dogs, a metal nail file or emery board to smooth out the clipped nails, and styptic powder and cotton balls in case you clip too close. Although many dog owners choose to have their vet or professional dog groomer trim their pet's nails, it is an expensive and time-consuming way to get the job done. There are four types of nail trimmer to choose from:

### Nail scissors

Each blade has a semicircular opening. When squeezed together they make a circular opening that can accommodate a dog's toenail. You simply insert the nail and snip, taking care not to cut too close to the quick or to a tiny blood vessel leading into the nail. If you cut too close it will cause slight bleeding.

### Safety nail trimmer

These resemble small pliers with a spring between the handles. They function as scissors but have a safety stop to limit the length of nail to cut.

### Guillotine trimmers

This trimming tool is a cross between a pair of pliers and a cigar cutter. The nail is placed in the hole at the end of the tool. The handles are squeezed together, causing a sharp blade to slide across, slicing off the exposed bit of nail. These seem to be the tool of choice for many veterinarians and professional groomers.

## ELECTRIC NAIL TRIMMER

Like an electric grinding wheel, it trims by sanding off the excess nail with a high-speed rotary head. Clipper attachments are available for grinding, sanding, or smoothing. All nail trimmers require caution when in use but the electric trimmer even more so. This tool may be the easiest to use because it takes the nail down in stages and gives you more opportunity to stop at the right place. All nail trimmers require patience and practice, however, and tender loving care.

## *Cleaning your dog's teeth*

Unclean teeth are not very pretty to look at, and they can be the cause of bad breath as well. More important, unwholesome teeth can be the cause of serious health problems leading to the need for medical treatment. Prevention is the first line of defense. This means maintaining clean teeth and healthy gums. Your dog's teeth should be part of a complete veterinary checkup, with dental problems taken care of at the time of the examination. In addition to veterinary dental care, home care is of vital importance for good looks, hygiene, and good health. Your first concern should be controlling the formation of plaque on the surface of the teeth, which consists of bacteria, various proteins, and food debris. Plaque control is aided by self-cleaning hard foods and chew toys.

But the most effective way of removing and preventing plaque buildup is by brushing your dog's teeth. Obtain a toothbrush that is designed for dogs, which should have soft, multitufted synthetic bristles. The tips should be rounded to avoid injuring sensitive gum tissue. There are also a number of cleverly designed devices for brushing a dog's teeth. They are almost all recommended. There are a number of canine toothpastes available. Do not use toothpaste formulated for humans. Remove the stains on the surface of the teeth with a wet washcloth by rubbing vigorously. Try not to force your dog's jaw open if he resists. Gently roll back his lips, enough to expose his teeth. Scrub the teeth by holding the toothbrush at a 45-degree angle at the gum surface. Make small circular motions brushing below the gum line as well as the entire tooth surface. Finish each tooth with a vertical motion so that the brush cleans between the teeth. Once all the teeth have been cleaned on the outer surface you must then clean the inner side as well. The dog may resist having the brush go inside his mouth. Try a temporary substitute, such as cotton-tipped applicators, gauze wrapped around your fingers, or other form of finger brushes. Brush your dog's teeth as often as possible, ideally twice a week.

### Getting rid of odors

Odors are often a barometer of your dog's health. A healthy, properly fed, and well-groomed dog will have few unpleasant odors coming from his body.

The so-called "doggie" smell is usually caused by an accumulation of dirt, saliva, and debris that have remained on the dog's coat too long. Heavy-coated dogs reek of this odor most often, and especially when the unbrushed coat gets wet. Daily brushing and an occasional bath are the best remedies.

Some odors are caused by medical conditions such as skin eruptions, ear infections, or impacted or infected anal glands. These require veterinary treatment. Bathing, daily brushing, and combing almost always help most odors caused by medical conditions. A number of odors cannot be eliminated until the dog is restored to normal good health. It is helpful to clean thoroughly or replace your dog's bedding after eliminating the source of his odor.

Flatulence, an unpleasant source of odor, is caused either by poorly balanced meals, parasites, or the dog's inability to properly digest what he has eaten. Flatulence is gas leaving the body caused by excess bacteria in the bowels. Sometimes a change in diet is the cause.

Mouth odor or bad breath can be caused by nasal ailments, gastric acid, poor digestion, or poorly balanced diets. Puppies develop bad breath if they are infested with roundworms. A worming treatment from a veterinarian usually solves this problem. Dental problems of every description are an important source of mouth odor. Tooth decay, gum diseases, tartar and plaque deposits on the surface of the teeth, and uncleaned teeth are all possible causes of mouth odor. The cure is obvious. Take care of the dental problem and you will be taking care of mouth odor.

Covering up the odor with perfume-type products of one sort or another is a poor substitute for ridding the smell at the source; the most effective way to deal with this is to neutralize or destroy the odor at the source. You can purchase an odor neutralizer at a pet supply store or through a mail-order catalog. There are many such products available. Some work and some don't. Ask for advice about the best product from a dog expert or from your retailer.

## Fifteen

# Your Dog's Health

**Y**ou are responsible for your pet's health. When a dog feels lousy he cannot pick up the phone and call his doctor. Dog-moms and dog-dads have to do it for him. At the first signs of illness you cannot say take two biscuits and call me in the morning. First, you must do what you can to keep him healthy, and then you must be able to recognize the signs that your dog is getting sick. At that point you should get medical attention for him. You should establish an active relationship with a local veterinarian so the dog can be looked after as quickly as possible. Choose a vet before your dog gets sick. Sooner or later everyone needs a doctor. Your dog is no different.

### How to choose the best veterinarian for your dog

Word of mouth is the most common approach to selecting a dog doctor, and it's not a bad way to do it. The experiences and opinions of dog owners with a specific veterinarian are valuable. Professional referrals are also a good way to find a vet. Do not hesitate to ask a dog trainer or professional groomer. Veterinary medical associations are yet another source, and they can be found in most phone books and on various search engines on the Internet. These associations are best able to direct you to a veterinarian close to you. When talking to a vet for the first time it is a good idea to ask how much he or she charges for various services. You should be able to discuss this openly. Cleanliness is a very important factor when choosing a vet. When you enter the office look around and see if it is neat and clean. Are members of the staff (including the doctor) wearing clean gowns, uniforms, or work clothes? Are the floors swept and mopped? Are animal "accidents" cleaned up quickly? How well does the vet relate to animals? Good veterinarians do not have to play with their patients; they do not even have to like animals. All that's necessary is that they respect you and your dog. He or she must be skilled and knowledgeable about current standards, practices, and advances in modern veterinary medicine. He or she must be sensitive to pain and suffering and have a humane approach to animals and their care. Look for diagnostic skill rather than becoming overly impressed with office decor and chrome-plated equipment. There are brilliantly intuitive doctors with a sixth sense about identifying what's wrong with your dog. Doctors with great diagnostic skill are outstanding and should be valued highly by any dog owner. See your vet at least once a year.

## The essentials of a proper veterinary examination

### EYES

The dog's eyes often reflect good or bad health. Anemia, infections, and jaundice may be discovered by an eye examination. The eyes sometimes have hard-to-see injuries or developing ulcers. Vets use an instrument called an ophthalmoscope to observe the inner structure of the eyes, especially the lens and retina. It is an instrument containing a perforated mirror and lenses. The vet will look for cataracts in older dogs as well as cloudy lenses or other symptoms of disease with this instrument.

### EARS

To examine the ear canal properly, the veterinarian uses an instrument called an otoscope. It is a tubular flashlight with a funnel at the end that is inserted in the dog's ear canal, which is deep and curved, protecting the inner ear. Ear infection is common in dogs and is detected by an unpleasant odor and the dog's tendency to shake and scratch its head. By looking into the wide end of the funnel the vet can get a better view of the ear canal and the organs within it. The vet should check all parts of the ear and ear flap for parasites, ulcers, infections, and foreign matter.

### Nose

A dog's nose is not the health barometer most people believe it to be. A healthy animal's nose may be hot, cold, wet, or dry. The veterinarian will check your dog's nose for discharges or other irregularities. He or she may also use a light to examine the nasal passage for seeds or plant particles that may have lodged there.

### Mouth

The condition of a dog's gums, tongue, and palate should be closely observed in a complete checkup. The color of the lining of the lips and gums is particularly important. The lack of a pink or red color in this area could indicate anemia. The vet will also check the mouth area for tumors, ulcers, or other abnormalities.

### Teeth

Oral hygiene is as important to dogs as it is to humans and should not be overlooked. Puppies may need help to remove their first teeth. Some vets use ultrasonic and other types of equipment that is the same as or very similar to that used in human dentistry. But, unlike humans, most dogs require sedation or anesthesia for thorough dental treatment including cleaning and scaling.

### Respiratory system

The examination of the mouth area continues with an evaluation of the larynx (voice box) and trachea, which is the pathway to the lungs. A stethoscope, which magnifies the sounds of the lungs, will be used as part of the screening process. The results of this screening will determine if further examinations or tests are required.

### SPINE/MUSCULOSKELETON

Your dog's gait or walk should be observed to spot any abnormalities of the pelvis. Using his or her sense of touch, a veterinarian will examine the dog's neck, backbone, and tail. The fleshy fat covering any muscle tone will be evaluated as part of the process.

### LEGS

The vet should examine the dog's limbs carefully by looking at them and feeling them. Close attention will be paid to the dog's joints for possible deformation, inflammation, or disease. The doctor also should check the feet and footpads closely for any inflammation, deformities, or embedded matter.

### SKIN

The skin is the largest organ of the body. The condition of it and the dog's hair coat are important health indicators. Part of the examination of the skin will include looking for evidence of fleas, ticks, and other parasites, tumors, wounds, and infections. The lymph nodes under the skin should also be checked. Some skin conditions require skin scrapings, tissue biopsies, or allergy tests to identify the problem. Laboratory analysis may be necessary.

### REPRODUCTIVE SYSTEM

The reproductive system should be checked for abnormalities. Your vet may suggest having your dog neutered for reasons other than birth control. For example, castrating male dogs reduces the incidence of prostate disease and some types of cancer. Neutering may also help eliminate or modify some behavioral problems such as aggressiveness or the tendency to roam. Spaying a female dog (ovariohysterectomy) reduces the possibility of a serious uterine infection (pyometra). Spaying also reduces or eliminates the incidence of breast cancer.

### ABDOMINAL CAVITY

The vet should use his or her hands to press, touch, and feel the abdomen for any excess fluids, gas, or tumors. The spleen, bladder, kidneys, intestines, and liver also should be evaluated. A male dog's enlarged prostate gland or a female's enlarged uterus, as well as other abnormalities, may be detected as part of the abdominal cavity exam.

### CARDIOVASCULAR SYSTEM

A stethoscope will be used to evaluate the heart. Any abnormal sounds or beats may lead to additional tests, such as X rays and electrocardiograms. X rays are important diagnostic tools but usually require sedation or anesthesia because it is almost impossible to get a dog to hold still for X rays that are not blurred by fidgeting.

### ANAL AREA

Dogs have small sacs on each side of the anal opening, and they may become enlarged or infected. This condition is referred to as "impacted anal glands." The sign is when the dog rubs his haunches along the floor in an attempt to relieve the discomfort. The veterinarian should be able to identify and treat this problem easily, and also note and evaluate any tumors that may be present.

### IMMUNIZATION

Getting your dog vaccinated with original and then booster shots is probably the most important aspect of your dog's annual veterinary examination. One of the greatest advances in helping animals live longer, more comfortable lives is the highly effective immunization against life-threatening diseases. Many inoculations are now given in one multiple injection to prevent several disease threats at the same time. Early immunizations of puppies and then a series of booster shots are recommended highly. After this you must bring your dog in at least once a year for the booster shots to continue the protection throughout the dog's life. Your veterinarian determines which vaccines are given, and that is based on the dangers in your region. The most common vaccines given to all dogs are for rabies, distemper, hepatitis, parainfluenza, leptospirosis, parvovirus, and, in some instances, Lyme disease.

### WHEN TO CALL THE VETERINARIAN
### IF YOUR DOG IS NOT WELL

Many inexperienced dog owners are often unsure about whether their dogs are seriously sick and require professional veterinary care. As with humans, many ailments are not serious and are taken care of by the body's ability to heal itself. On occasion, however, the average dog may become seriously sick and should be checked by a professional before the situation deteriorates. To help you decide when to call and ask for help or information, here is a list of medical signs to watch for. If your dog has one or more of these, do not hesitate to call your veterinarians and ask for an opinion.

- excessive coughing, sneezing, or snorting
- frequent wheezing, running nose, gagging
- hoarseness
- moaning, crying, or whimpering
- repeated vomiting
- excessive and sudden appetite
- excessive and sudden thirst
- unusual or prolonged lack of appetite
- unusual lack of thirst
- inability to eat food or drink water
- unusual slobbering
- abnormally pale gums
- foul breath
- difficulty breathing (labored breathing)
- constant shaking of the head
- dizziness
- convulsions
- paralysis
- limping
- trembling and shivering
- sudden weight loss
- excessive shedding as an abnormal condition

- swellings, lumps, sore spots, especially on the abdomen
- rampant diarrhea
- cloudy urine
- uncontrollable urination
- odorous urine
- gritty or sandy urine
- dark yellow or orange urine

## The most common life-threatening diseases of dogs

### RABIES

Rabies is a fatal disease threatening all warm-blooded animals, including humans, and is highly contagious. A virus existing in the saliva of infected animals causes it. The usual mode of transmission is through a bite from a rabid animal in which the saliva containing the virus enters the victim's body. The rabies virus also can enter the body through contact with an open wound or scratch, although it is less common. Once the virus enters the body it eventually travels to nerve endings. Over a period of time it advances to the spinal cord and eventually makes its way up to the brain, where it causes degeneration of the entire nervous system. It produces altered behavior, paralysis, and death. The incubation period between entry of the virus into the body and the first signs of the disease varies from one week to one year. In North America infected skunks, raccoons, foxes, and bats most frequently carry rabies.

Contrary to widespread opinion, rats, mice, squirrels, chipmunks, guinea pigs, and most other rodents are not involved in any significant numbers. The only rodent of importance in rabies transmission appears to be the woodchuck, or groundhog. Of the domestic animals, only dogs and cats are important carriers of the virus. Clinical signs of rabies take two forms: the "furious" stage and the paralytic or "dumb" stage. In dogs the furious stage may last from one to seven days and is characterized by restlessness, nervousness, and the onset of biting behavior. Infected dogs may snap and nip involuntarily and certainly will bite anyone that approaches and consequently infect that person. As the disease progresses the dog will turn on its family because of sensitivity to being touched, along with sensitivity to light. In this stage the dog is oblivious to pain, will howl or cry, lose all appetite, drool, and chew on its leash or other restraints, including the bars of its wire crate. The paralytic stage lasts for one or two days and the signs are obvious.

It is of life and death importance not to touch or even go near such a dog for fear of being infected with the deadly virus. Just a passing scrape of the hand along the dog's teeth can cause infection. The course of rabies in human beings is similar to those of animal victims of the disease. *Therefore, with few exceptions, public health experts feel strongly that rabid dogs must be dealt with by professionals only and humanely destroyed.* Even a healthy dog that has bitten a human being should be confined for at least ten days and observed for the development of clinical signs of rabies.

Treatment for rabid dogs is never recommended. Treatment for human beings exposed to a rabid animal does exist but must begin as soon as humanly possible if it is going to be effective. *The most important thing that can be done when bitten by a dog, rabid or not, is to immediately flush and cleanse the bite with soap and water as thoroughly as possible to prevent a virus or bacteria from entering the bloodstream, and to report the incident to your physician.* Rabies is effectively preventable by having your dog vaccinated for this gruesome disease.

## CANINE DISTEMPER

This is a life-threatening disease for all dogs that have not been vaccinated for it. Pets of all ages may come down with canine distemper, but dogs under stress, puppies, and those that have never had follow-up booster vaccinations every year are the most susceptible. The incubation period is six to nine days, but because the early signs are very subtle, symptoms may not be apparent for two to three weeks.

Distemper symptoms appear at first like an upper-respiratory ailment similar to a flu virus in a human. Dry coughs, loss of appetite, running nose, watery eyes, fever, and depression are signs of this serious ailment. Advance stage signs may include diarrhea, a hypersensitivity to light, and convulsions. It is a difficult disease to diagnose. There is no doubt that these symptoms require the immediate services of a veterinarian whether the dog actually has canine distemper or not. Faithfully follow your veterinarian's instructions, but prevention is the only real help. Immunization early in the puppy's life plus annual booster shots offers the best hope.

### INFECTIOUS CANINE HEPATITIS

Vets refer to this as ICH. It is a life-threatening viral disease that can infect dogs of all ages because it is highly contagious, as are most forms of hepatitis. The virus is transmitted from all body secretions of carrier dogs, and in the urine of dogs several months after they recover. The virus can enter the body of a dog only by ingestion. This form of hepatitis has no relationship to hepatitis in humans and is not transmitted between dog and human in either direction. The incubation period lasts from five to nine days with varying signs. The dog's temperature rises from a normal 101.5 degrees F (average) to 104 degrees F, which may last for six days. The signs of ICH are depression, apathy, abnormal thirst, loss of appetite, and excess watering of the eyes and nose. Diarrhea, vomiting, spasm, and heavy and rapid breathing are also signs of this painful disease. Because it localizes in the dog's liver, he may arch his back or rub his stomach area to relieve pain.

Immediate medical attention is necessary. Your dog's recovery depends on you following your veterinarian's instructions. You may be asked to leave the dog with the veterinarian for several days. Infectious canine hepatitis is sometimes combined with canine distemper. Early immunization and boosters are important.

### CANINE PARVOVIRUS ENTERITIS

The most common type of parvovirus is the intestinal form. Its most likely victims are puppies, young dogs, and old dogs whose lives are threatened once the infection enters their body. Transmission is achieved through direct contact with infected dogs or with the feces of infected dogs. The dog's age, state of health, and how soon it receives medical attention determine whether or not the infected dog survives. The signs of this life-threatening disease are depression, incessant and grievous vomiting, bloody diarrhea and scouring (loss of intestinal lining), elevated fever, loss of appetite, and severe dehydration.

When these signs appear the dog must be rushed to a veterinarian as quickly as possible if it is to have any chance for survival. Death can ensue within two to four days. Treatment is mostly supportive, involving intravenous fluids and antibiotics (to prevent secondary infections). The only means of recovery involves allowing the dog's immune system to fight off the virus as lost fluids are replaced. One cannot emphasize too much the importance of replacing lost fluids either by drinking or through intravenous injection. Vaccination against parvovirus is essential. The age a puppy is vaccinated for parvovirus is critical. When given too young the vaccine fails. If given too late, the virus may have already infected the body. Consult your veterinarian about when to vaccinate for parvovirus.

# Sixteen

# *Pests and Parasites*

**A**lmost all dogs sooner or later serve as hosts for either internal or external parasites. An internal parasite is usually a worm or wormlike organism that manages to enter the body of the dog, take up residence, derive sustenance from either blood or tissue, multiply, and then leave. An external parasite lives in various ways on the outer surface of the dog's body, feeds on blood and tissue, multiplies, and then leaves. They too are parasitic but are pests in the sense that external parasites cause a dog misery with irritation and itching. All parasites are a serious threat to the well-being of your dog. These creatures feed off the bodies of their hosts, damage the body's tissue, and often cause secondary infections and some serious conditions such as anemia. Pests and parasites are often the subject of humor, but there is nothing funny about them. They are your dog's enemy. Many of them are your enemy as well, as several are transmittable to humans. They must be detected by their early signs and eradicated from the dog's body and the immediate environment. This involves medical attention, sanitation, fumigation, and specially prescribed home care instructions from a veterinarian. Parasites should be considered a serious health threat.

### The nature of internal parasites

Internal parasites are the most common ailments of dogs. Almost all internal parasites that collect in a dog's body are called worms. Worms vary in kind, size, effect, and seriousness to the health of the dog. Although all worms can do harm to the dog's body, with early detection and treatment few create permanent or irreparable damage. Depending on the degree of infestation, the condition runs from mild to gravely serious. The early signs include a lethargic manner, inconsistent appetite, diarrhea, and blood in the stool (a serious sign). The signs of heavy infestation are weight loss, bloated stomach, loss of fluid, dry and thinning coat, constant drowsiness, and, in some cases, anemia. The most common sign of parasitic infestation is loss of energy. The dog does not seem to be himself. When you suspect that your dog or puppy is infected, take a stool sample to your veterinarian for specific diagnosis and treatment. Because worms may not appear in every stool it is best to collect small specimens of from one to five stools (collected every other day) and bring the material to the vet for microscopic examination. In most cases treatment is uncomplicated and effective.

### *The most common internal parasites*
#### ROUNDWORMS (ASCARIDS)

Most puppies younger than six months of age are infected with roundworms. Nursing puppies can acquire them from their mother's milk. On occasion they are found in adult dogs. These are long worms that reach four to eight inches in length; are white and cylindrical in shape; and are often seen in the dog's stool. They are the most common species of internal parasite in dogs. They can be passed to humans and are particularly harmful to young children who may be contaminated as a result of handling infested pets.

#### HOOKWORMS

Hookworms are thick, round worms that are less than an inch long that thrive in the small intestine of the adult dog and are passed through the stool. The adults hook themselves onto the wall of the host animal's intestine and ingest blood. If not treated the dog will eventually develop anemia. The eggs are microscopic in size and cannot be identified specifically without a laboratory stool analysis.

#### WHIPWORMS

These serious parasites are somewhat difficult to detect. They are very small worms that settle in the dog's colon and intestinal tract. Once whipworm eggs are ingested by the dog they remain within from larvae to adults and for as long as sixteen months. During that period, the host dog slowly loses blood with accompanying loss of weight. Diarrhea becomes frequent, with evidence of blood in the stool. Diagnosis is made by microscopic examination of the stool. Treatment is usually effective but reinfestation is common.

## HEARTWORMS

This is one of the most serious of all the parasitic infestations. Heartworms are large worms that lodge in the right side of the heart and in the pulmonary vessels of the lung. They make it much harder for the heart to pump blood to the lungs, which in effect ages and weakens it. They infect dogs through the bite of a mosquito that has bitten an infected dog previously. The symptoms are exhaustion, coughing, loss of weight despite good diet and appetite, and labored breathing. Without proper treatment these parasites lead to heart failure and death. Prevention is the best cure. Keep your dog away from mosquitoes. If that is not possible, ask your veterinarian about heartworm prevention pills. They are harmful if the dog is infested already. A blood test is necessary before use of these pills to ensure that your dog is free of the parasite.

## TAPEWORMS

One form of this parasite is potentially contagious to humans (the *Echinococcus* type) and very uncommon. The tapeworm is comprised of a head equipped with hooks and suckers that enable it to affix to the intestinal wall as it progressively grows into a long chain of segments. Occasionally several segments pass into the stool, but the head always remains to form new links. Infection can sometimes take a long time to detect. It can begin as digestive upsets, irregular appetite, weight loss, stomach discomfort, and poor coat condition. Diagnosis is made through examination of fecal matter, although this is not always effective. The most common source of tapeworm is fleas. You cannot rid your dog of these parasites without ridding his environment of fleas. Your dog also can get tapeworms by eating infected, uncooked meat, either in the wild or from the kitchen, or from raw fish. Lice also can carry the infection. Contact with intermediate hosts such as mice, rats, squirrels, and rabbits must be avoided. Treatment involves destroying the head within the host's body. The services of a veterinarian are crucial for a successful cure.

### The nature of external parasites

If dogs have true enemies, it would have to be external parasites such as fleas, flies, ticks, lice, and mites that are the carriers of disease, allergies, internal parasites, irritation, and misery. When a dog's body is invaded by external parasites a vet can best determine what the pests are and how to treat them. The signs may be scratching, head shaking, pacing, restlessness, hair loss, and visible movement of parasites in the coat and on the body. Many veterinarians have staff and facilities for bathing dogs and administering flea and tick dips. Removing embedded ticks may be too harrowing for some dog owners who would rather have the chore taken care of by a professional. The best treatment for internal and external parasites is a good prevention-control attitude. If a dog becomes infested with parasites it is not enough to kill and remove them from the body. All areas that the dog inhabits must be cleaned thoroughly with soap and water and attacked with a proper pesticide. If this is not done the dog is certain to become infested again and again. All external parasites can and will attach themselves to humans if given the opportunity. That is why it is essential to treat the dog and his environment at the earliest sign of infestation.

## *The most common external parasites*
### FLEAS

These are the number one cause of skin disease in dogs and are also responsible for the transmission of tapeworms. Some dogs develop allergies to substances found in flea saliva. Fleas cause misery for dogs and are extremely difficult to remove from the environment. The flea actually spends only a small portion of its life cycle feeding off a dog's blood. Most of its time is spent in the environment, which is probably your home. Flea-infested dogs become restless, may lose weight, and can damage their coats by biting and scratching. Dog owners may be bitten by fleas and develop skin rashes themselves. The bites can cause inflammation of the skin at the site of the bite. The constant scratching causes the hair to break and creates bald spots.

Some dogs have allergic reactions to flea bites, which results in severe dermatitis. The first aspect of solving the problem is to treat the dog's environment, both indoors and outdoors. Spray or dust his sleeping area with products recommended by a veterinarian or an experienced dog person. Once the environment has been treated, give the dog a bath using a flea shampoo and a dip. Apply a flea collar or douse the dog with a good flea powder every night for two or three weeks, until the situation is under control. Treating your pet for fleas without simultaneously treating the environment is both inefficient and ineffective. Fleas are your dog's enemy.

### LICE

Lice are wingless insects that exist where fleas are allowed to breed. Although rare, they do occur on dogs and spend their entire lives on one host or animal. When a dog begins scratching, biting, and rubbing, it is quite possible that he has lice. The principal difference between lice and fleas is that lice remain in one spot and dig in. They are the smallest part of an inch and extremely difficult to see. Lice are small black insects that live on the dog's body and take blood meals. If the dog scratches hard, these tiny insects burrow in deeper. Unlike fleas, lice lay their eggs on the dog's coat by attaching them firmly to the hairs. The lice eggs are called nits and have light-colored, waxy bodies. If infestation is great, the lice can cause a considerable blood loss, resulting in anemia. Lice are eliminated by a bath with an insecticide shampoo obtained from a veterinarian.

## Ticks

Ticks are parasites that feed off the blood of their hosts, robbing them of their vitality and spreading disease. The hard tick variety are carriers of Rocky Mountain spotted fever, Q fever, and other more rare diseases. The soft tick variety is a prolific carrier of spirochetes, which cause Lyme disease, now considered the most common tick-carried disease in North America. The disease is transmitted by the minuscule deer tick, found in the northeastern United States, the Northwest, California, and in a number of countries throughout the world. The most prolific tick is the American dog tick, one of the hard tick varieties. Another is the wood tick. American dog ticks live inside your house and kennel. They infect dogs at all times of the year. Wood ticks infect dogs only in their adult stage and do not infect the house or kennel. Their bites cause irritation and loss of blood. When a tick is pulled away from the dog's skin after it has become attached, a small amount of tissue also will be pulled away. This causes a blood smear and sometimes swelling. An antiseptic or antibacterial medication applied topically is important to prevent infection. Some ticks can produce fever, paralysis, and even death. Although dogs seldom develop fatal diseases from ticks, tick diseases can be transmitted to humans. To control ticks in your environment it is important to understand that they live in one place and feed in another. You must spray both inside and outside your home with a tick-specific pesticide. Spray the entire outer environment, paying particular attention to the areas where the dog spends most of his time. Inside the home, spray every conceivable crack and crevice where they may hide, including baseboards, closets, clothing, and furniture. Look for ticks throughout the hair coat of your dog. Favorite hiding places are inside the dog's ears and between the toes. Although a flea and tick shampoo is helpful, a tick dip is the most effective remedy to remove them from the body.

### *Removing a tick.*

If a female tick is dug into the skin and is in the process of engorging, it is important to remove it. First, put a drop or two of alcohol on the body. It will serve as an antiseptic and help loosen the grip. Using a tweezers, grasp the tick as close to the skin as possible. Twist the body in a counterclockwise direction as you pull it out. This will help prevent the head from breaking off and remaining in the skin. Dispose of it by dropping it in a container of alcohol. Use an alcohol swab to clean the wound or dab it with an antibiotic ointment. See your vet.

## MITES

These organisms are almost microscopic in size and barely visible to the naked eye. Mites are arachnids, part of the same family as spiders, with many species, several of which create problems for dogs. They are not insects.

Several of the many species of mites are medically injurious to dogs, among which are the *Demodex* mites (cause of demodectic mange), canine scabies (cause of sarcoptic mange), and *Otodectes cynotis* (ear mite infection). Demodectic mange is a serious parasitic skin disease involving several areas of hair loss, mostly near or on the head and front legs. The infected skin becomes red and scaly. It is a treatable condition. Intense itching, hair loss, and crusting of the skin characterize sarcoptic mange. It is usually found on the ears, front legs, chest, and abdomen. It often leads to secondary bacterial or yeast infections. Demodectic and sarcoptic mange mites must be identified under a microscope. A scraping of skin is taken from the dog for examination. Ear mites are more commonly found in cats but do afflict dogs as well. They are detectable by the formation of dark, crusty material in the ear canals along with a foul odor. They cause ear scratching and rubbing, as well as head shaking. A veterinarian must treat mites and the disorders they cause. Mites and their accompanying medical problems may be transmitted to humans.

# Seventeen

# *How to Save Your Dog's Life* (First Aid)

$A$*s* in human medicine, emergencies require quick, resourceful action, and you may not have time to get professional help for the lifesaving procedures. First aid is exactly what the term implies. The following procedures are temporary but essential so that life can be saved, irreparable damage avoided, and the animal spared as much pain as possible.

### *The first-aid kit*

A sensible first-aid kit can make the difference between life and death. The items on the following list will cover most emergencies. Or you may prefer to purchase a preassembled kit designed for pet owners.

These are available in pet supply catalogs or on pet supply web sites on the Internet. We suggest you stock your kit with the following items:

- a first-aid box or bag that is clearly marked
- gauze bandage rolls in both wide and extrawide sizes
- small, medium, and large gauze pads for applying directly to a wound
- adhesive tape
- cotton swabs
- absorbent cotton balls
- scissors
- tweezers
- tongue depressors
- rectal thermometer
- soft muzzle with Velcro fastener
- Vaseline
- antibiotic ointment
- antiseptic powder or spray
- aromatic spirits of ammonia
- mineral oil
- Kaopectate
- Pepto Bismol
- hydrogen peroxide
- eye ointment
- activated charcoal (for absorbing poison)
- styptic powder (to stop minor bleeding)
- ipecac (to induce vomiting)
- a card or sheet with the name, address, and phone number of your veterinarian

### *In the event of an emergency*

#### BE PREPARED

Know in advance whom to contact for twenty-four-hour emergency veterinary service. Read and learn the following first-aid and emergency treatment procedures beforehand so you are familiar with the signs of emergent conditions.

#### HOW TO APPROACH AN INJURED DOG

Animals that are frightened or in pain may try to bite or maul you, so protect yourself. The use of a muzzle is best for this purpose.

#### RESTRAINT

A dog can be restrained by wrapping him in a blanket or coat. Use a leash if possible. If the dog will not allow you to hook the leash to the collar, or if he is not wearing a collar, run the end of the leash through the hand loop and form a lasso. It will be much easier for you to get this around the dog's neck without being bitten.

#### THE MUZZLE

If the dog's breathing appears normal, use the soft muzzle from your first-aid kit or tie his mouth shut with gauze bandage to avoid getting bitten. A dog in pain will snap or bite hard if you touch a painful part of his body. If you do not have a muzzle, make one with gauze, string, your belt, or your necktie. Make a loop or half-knot and slip it over the dog's nose, halfway up. Pull it until it tightens. Bring the ends under the jaw, forming another half-knot. Secure the ends behind the dog's ears with a bowknot, as you would tie a shoelace. Do not muzzle too tightly. It may be necessary to tie the front paws (if not injured). With this done you can examine the dog safely.

### If your dog is not breathing

Stay calm, talk softly, and maintain a soothing manner. Remove the dog from harm's way if he is on the road or in the middle of the street. Be certain he is breathing. If his ribs do not expand and contract, if he is unconscious, if his skin is cool and pale-looking he has probably stopped breathing. Clear his airway. Straighten his neck and extend his tongue. Remove any apparent obstructions or thick wads of mucous with a handkerchief or gauze pad. Administer canine artificial respiration: Hold the dog's mouth closed tight. Place his nose in your own mouth and blow in at a steady pace for several seconds. Stop for a few seconds to see if he has exhaled on his own. If he is still not breathing repeat the procedure and keep repeating it until he begins to breathe on his own. If he does his ribs will expand and contract. Do not give up, as it may take as long as a half hour to get him breathing again.

### If your dog is bleeding

External bleeding is obvious. It comes from wounds. Excessive blood loss must be prevented and infection avoided.

Superficial wounds show slight blood loss. Wash

the wound with soap and water and apply an antiseptic or an antibiotic ointment. Smear on a light film of Vaseline and cover with a gauze pad and tape. For persistent bleeding, it may be necessary to use a pressure bandage. For this, apply a gauze pad large enough to cover the wound and bind it tightly around several times in order to create pressure over the bleeding cut. Cover the pad completely with adhesive tape. If no tape is available, tie the pad with gauze or cloth strips torn down the center and knotted at the ends.

Severe or deep cuts are serious. A severed artery shows light red blood rushing quickly. Dark-colored blood that flows slowly is from a vein. These types of lacerations or punctures extend beyond the skin into the tissue beneath. Place a gauze pad over the wound and apply pressure with your hand for several minutes, allowing the blood to collect on the dressing and clot. If the blood soaks through, keep applying one pad on top of another. Maintain pressure on the wound. Wrap completely with bandage and cover the entire bandage with tape. Get professional help immediately.

### If your dog goes into shock

Severe fright, traumatizing injury, or internal bleeding may cause shock, which is a state of collapse caused by a failure of peripheral circulation. The signs of shock are empty staring into space, prostration, weak pulse, shallow but rapid breathing, panting, temperature 100 degrees F or lower, unconsciousness, cool extremities, pale gums and tongue. To prevent shock, bleeding must be arrested, pain relieved, and infection prevented. Reassure the dog, talking quietly as you might to a frightened child, and help preserve the dog's body heat with a blanket (no electrical appliances). Keep him quiet and rush him to a veterinarian.

### If your dog has a broken leg

The signs of a broken leg are loss of the ability to bear body weight, limping, localized pain with swelling, obvious deformity, abnormal angulation, or the protrusion of bone through the skin.

#### WHAT TO DO FOR A BROKEN LEG

Muzzle the dog immediately. Restrain him as gently as possible. Immobilize the injured area with a splint. Improvise if you must with any firm object such as a small plank of wood, a tree branch, heavy cardboard, even a tool such as a hammer. The splint must be long enough to immobilize the entire leg. It is best if you can pad the surface of the splint with a towel or soft garment so that it is soft on the dog's skin. Tie the leg to the splint securely with gauze, string, or rope. Use adhesive tape. It is best to wrap the entire splint so the leg cannot move, but do not hamper circulation by making it too tight. Treat the dog for shock and rush to a veterinarian for professional treatment. *Do not attempt to set the bone yourself. There is little or nothing that can be done by you if your dog has fractured a rib, his skull, or any part of his back. These require emergency, professional care. Do not use a splint for these types of fractures.*

### If your dog is burned

Most burns are caused by fire, electricity, friction, corrosive chemicals, or hot liquid. They singe the hair, cause the skin to turn red, create intense pain, and may turn the skin white or black if severe enough. The most common burns come from scalding hot water or other kitchen liquids, such as hot soup or coffee spilling onto the dog. To treat burns of this type, first muzzle the dog and then restrain him gently with a towel wrapped around the unburned area. Almost all burns continue to damage the tissue beneath the skin because of the ongoing heat. Therefore, the most important thing is to lower the temperature of the burned area with cold water or cold towels soaked in ice water. The sooner the area is cooled, the less tissue is damaged. Cool the burned area for at least twenty minutes or longer.

One of the great dangers of a serious burn is infection because of the loss of protective skin. To prevent this apply a thick film of antibiotic ointment to the wound, such as Bacitracin or Neosporin, and bandage over it with a thick covering of gauze pads and rolled gauze. *Do not use home remedies such as butter or lard.* Look for signs of shock, breathing difficulties, or coughing, and get to a vet quickly. If the burn is caused by a chemical or household product such as drain cleaner or lye, flush the burned area liberally with cool to tepid water and coat it with antibiotic ointment. Get immediate veterinary help. Electrical burns are usually around the mouth where the dog has bitten into a live wire. The area will be injured seriously and red in color. Electrical burns often interfere with the regular beat of the heart and could cause panting and breathing difficulties. You must treat the dog for shock and get to a veterinarian immediately.

## *If your dog is poisoned*

Poisons vary in type and effect and require a number of different therapies and antidotes. Poison may be inhaled, swallowed, or absorbed through the skin.

The signs of poisoning are sudden onset of severe illness: retching, abdominal tenderness, trembling, convulsions, vomiting, diarrhea, dilated or pin-point pupils, salivation, labored breathing, uncontrolled bleeding, weakness, or collapse.

### WHAT TO DO

Try to determine what the poison was, when it was ingested, and the amount swallowed. Call your veterinarian or the nearest poison control center. Tell your veterinarian your dog's age, any medical problems, if he is taking medication, and whether or not he has vomited since swallowing the poison. If possible, bring the material in its container (or at least the label) to the vet with the dog. See poison control information in the next paragraph.

### IF THE TOXIN IS ON THE SKIN

As a first-aid measure you can flush the area with copious amounts of water, then gently lather the skin with a mild soap and water. Never use turpentine or other poisonous substances to remove paint, tar, asphalt, or oil from your dog. Vegetable or mineral oil rubbed into the fur or on the skin may loosen the material before it hardens. Cornstarch or flour can then be used to absorb the substance before brushing it out of the fur or wiping it off the skin. Follow this with additional treatments and a bath in mild soapy water. Dried paint can be clipped from the hair coat. Some poisons must be expelled from inside the body by inducing vomiting with syrup of ipecac. **You must not induce vomiting** if you suspect that the poison is a strong acid or alkali, strychnine, a petroleum distillate, if the animal is unconscious, or if the signs of poisoning are already apparent. Milk or water may be given in most cases to wash the esophagus and to delay the absorption of the poison. **For the best advice available call the ASPCA National Animal Poison Control Center at 1-800-548-2423.** They are available to handle emergencies twenty-four hours a day, seven days a week. There is a charge payable by credit card. Veterinarians and toxicologists are available for consultation. For nonemergency information about pesticides that affect animals and humans there is the National Pesticide Telecommunications Network (NPTN) at 1-800-858-7378. The service will answer most questions concerning pesticides and how they affect animals and humans. It is available from 6:30 A.M. to 4:30 P.M., Pacific Time, seven days a week.

### *If your dog has heat exhaustion (leading to heat stroke)*

Almost any dog is susceptible to heat exhaustion and then heat stroke given the proper incitement, which is overexercising in hot, humid weather without access to shade and cool water. Overexposure to the sun in such weather is enough for some dogs to bring about this life-threatening condition. The most common cause is being confined in a car in hot weather. Older dogs, overweight dogs, puppies, dogs with heart or respiratory conditions, or dogs with short, pushed-in faces such as Bulldogs or Boxers are more susceptible to heat exhaustion than others. The signs are rapid breathing, loud panting, weakness, vomiting, muscle cramps, collapse, or unconsciousness. Dogs suffering from heat exhaustion may not show radically high body temperature. Heat stroke, however, is characterized by abnormally high internal temperature. Normal rectal temperature for a dog ranges between 100.5 degrees F to 102 degrees F. It is not uncommon for the temperature of a dog suffering heat stroke to rise above 108 degrees F, which is when cell damage begins to occur. Emergency treatment consists of getting the dog into an air-conditioned or cool, shady area. It is essential to reduce body temperature. This is accomplished by gently hosing the dog or soaking him in a partly filled tub of cool water. Do not use ice unless the body temperature has risen above 108 degrees F. Allow the cool water to evaporate on the surface of the body with moving air. Use a fan for this if possible. Monitor the dog's temperature with a rectal thermometer. The dog should receive veterinary care shortly after his temperature has been reduced.

### If your dog has gastric torsion ("bloat")

This is a life-threatening emergency that requires immediate veterinary care. The condition has two primary aspects: gastric dilation and volvulus. Gastric dilation involves the stomach's stretching and swelling rapidly with air or gas, as well as fluids, that it cannot expel. Volvulus involves the stomach's severely twisting at both ends, which accelerates the accumulation of gas dangerously, cutting off blood circulation, dislocating surrounding organs, and promoting severe bacterial infection. Bloat is more common in large- and giant-size breeds with deep chests such as German Shepherd Dogs, Great Danes, Saint Bernards, and Irish Setters. It is often brought about by strenuous activity immediately following a meal. Signs of the condition are abdominal enlargement caused by distention and twisting of the stomach. It is painful to the touch and can be accompanied by drooling, depression, restlessness, attempts at vomiting and defecating, labored breathing, pale gums, collapse, and unconsciousness often leading to death. Treatment involves immediate emergency care from a veterinarian who will take X rays and then attempt to expel the trapped gas and fluids by inserting a tube into the stomach through the mouth.

## Eighteen

# On the Road
# with Rover

**W**hat do you do with the family dog if you're going on a vacation or business trip? You can always include him in your travel plans and add a happiness factor to your trip if you're willing to do it the right way. It can be done easily even though it will involve extra effort and a few precautions. If you think about it, though, leaving a dog behind involves just as much effort and concern as taking him with you. There are a number of benefits to having your dog with you while traveling. Dogs are great traveling companions because they are good company and fun to be with. As long as he is with you there will be no need to worry about how he's doing. You will be sparing him from loneliness, boredom, or the feelings of loss once you do not come home on the first night away. Most dogs travel well and remain in good condition, physically and emotionally, as long as they are with you. There may be some inconveniences, but they are little compared to the advantages and benefits. Bone voyage.

### See your veterinarian before you leave

Good planning is the key to enjoying the pleasure of your dog's company. Here is a pretrip checklist.

- Make sure your dog is given a thorough medical checkup before leaving on any extended trip. Of course, this applies no matter how you travel and whether or not your dog stays home or goes with you.
- Have all vaccination and booster shots brought up-to-date. Tell your vet where you plan to go so that he can inoculate for that specific location.
- Inquire about the use of heartworm medication to be given prior to your trip.
- Obtain a medical certificate indicating that your dog has been given a proper veterinary examination and is in a good state of health.
- Ask your vet for a written medical history, including your dog's vaccination record.
- Ask for a rabies vaccination tag and a refill of current prescriptions, including tranquilizers if required.

### *Your dog's ID*

If your dog gets away from you on the trip your chances of recovering him are increased considerably if you place a quality collar on his neck and hook a metal ID tag onto it. The tag should be engraved with your name, the phone number of someone who is home to answer the call (don't forget the area code), and the words "Reward If Returned." A dog license tag from your community is another useful form of ID and should also be hooked onto the collar. If a lost dog ends up in a dog pound or shelter, his license will help you to recover him. You may find that you must prove your lost dog belongs to you. The solution here is have your dog tattooed on his underside or inner thigh with a code number provided by a dog registering company such as the National Dog Registering Company: Dial 1-800-NDR-DOGS or e-mail *info@natldogregistry.com.* Another effective lost dog service is IDPet. An alternative form of ID is to have your dog microchipped. A veterinarian injects a tiny microchip under the dog's skin. The chip is about the size of a grain of rice and contains an ID number that can be retrieved with a scanner. The registration number must be registered with the American Kennel Club to be effective for recovering a lost dog. Being able to have your lost dog identified and proven to belong to you is essential if you are going to take him with you on vacation.

### WHAT TO TAKE WHEN TRAVELING BY CAR

- Obtain a quality leather or nylon dog collar that fastens with a buckle or a Velcro fastener. You

must have a sturdy leash to control your dog. For
most dogs we recommend one made of leather
that is five-eighths of an inch wide and six feet
long. Hotels that allow pets may not allow a dog
to enter the premises unless he is held on a leash.

- Take your dog's regular food and water bowls
  along with you if it is practical.
- Be a good citizen and have with you at all times
  cleanup materials such as paper towels, plastic
  bags, and scoopers.
- Pack a complete supply of your dog's regular
  food. Do not rely on being able to purchase the
  same brand on the road. If you switch food on a
  trip it could upset your dog's stomach and cause
  diarrhea.
- Take along a plastic gallon of fresh water.
- Consider using a flea collar. Ask your vet if it is
  appropriate for your dog.
- Bring along a collapsible wire dog crate that is
  sized properly for your dog. It should have just
  enough room for the dog to stand up in and turn
  around and not much more. This will keep him
  safe while traveling and controlled while in a hotel room alone. Some dog crates are designed
  with a slanted front in order to fit into a hatch-
  back vehicle or station wagon.
- An essential for car travel is a seat belt designed
  for dogs, or a harness, both of which are designed for use with conventional seat belts. It is
  an important safety feature that will help you secure your dog in a moving car.

- Have a few photos of your dog for identification purposes if he becomes lost.
- When traveling in hot weather, keep a supply of ice cubes in a travel cooler. These can be useful for preventing heat exhaustion, heat prostration, or even heat stroke.
- Take along a first-aid and medicine kit containing: prescribed medications, a first-aid book, 3 percent hydrogen peroxide, activated charcoal tablets (for absorbing ingested poison), antibacterial ointment (for cuts and open wounds), Pepto Bismol (for diarrhea and upset stomachs), gauze bandages, gauze dressing pads, adhesive tape, a rectal thermometer, cotton tips, and tweezers.
- Don't forget your dog's grooming tools, such as his comb, brush, and dry shampoo.
- Bring his favorite toys, chewy things, his bed, and other prized possessions.

### *Car safety*

Whether the car is in motion or parked, secure your dog in a wire crate or with a seat belt and harness. Have your dog on his leash, in case you have to open the car door for any reason. Most dogs will try to run out of an open car door and that can certainly lead to a lost dog or a dog hit by a moving vehicle. Practice training him to stay when you open the door to avoid this situation.

In hot weather use the car's ventilation system or air conditioner to keep the dog comfortable and safe from heat prostration. Never leave your dog alone in a parked car. The sun is quite likely to heat up your car's interior to 120 degrees in fewer than three minutes, especially if the windows are closed, or even partially closed. Not even parking in the shade prevents the heat buildup. A dog left behind in a parked car may suffer from heat prostration, leading to heat stroke and eventual death. A dog alone in a parked car can either get himself into all kinds of trouble or be the victim of theft. Stealing pets and selling them illegally to eager buyers is not out of the question. Take your dog with you when you leave the car or have someone stay behind with him.

Every time you stop the car for any reason offer your dog an opportunity to drink some water and to relieve himself. After each stop allow as much time as possible between feeding time and the resumption of your trip. Ideally, allow six hours or more between feeding and traveling, particularly if your dog gets car sick easily.

Feed your dog lightly when traveling and give him his main meal at the end of the day, once you have stopped driving for the day. On hot days give your dog an ice cube to chew on.

### Traveling by train, bus, and boat

No train or bus lines in the United States allow animals of any kind to travel on board their conveyances, with the exception of guide dogs for the blind and service dogs for the disabled. Passenger ships may vary in their animal policies. Consult your travel agent or shipping line directly for their pet travel rules.

### *Traveling by plane*

Shipping a dog by air is never without some risk. There is always the possibility that the dog, who travels as freight, may miss his connecting flight and be forced to remain in his crate in a hangar or on the edge of the runway until another flight is available. He may go hungry, thirsty, and be given no opportunity to leave the crate to relieve himself. Additionally, if the flight or ground crew is indifferent, the dog may get too cold or too hot. Nevertheless, traveling by air with a dog is fast and economical, but requires advance planning. Check with individual airlines for their requirements and suggestions. Ask a savvy travel agent or travel club counselor for information about shipping your dog by air. Airlines do have strict requirements for the type of shipping crates used for this purpose. They may sell or rent one to you. Ask a vet about the use of a tranquilizer. Feed your dog lightly, six hours before flight time, and do not give him water within an hour or two of the flight time (except in hot weather). Give the dog a good run before crating him or tranquilizing him.

Plan the flight so he does not arrive on a weekend, a holiday, or during nonbusiness hours. Try to book a nonstop flight with no layovers, if possible. During the summer months, evening flights will be the most comfortable for the dog. Put his name on the crate so the ground crew can say hello to him. It may help ease his fear. If you are flying with him, ask the flight attendant to confirm that he is on board before leaving the gate for each connection.

### Hotels and motels

Never assume that hotels or motels automatically will allow you to rent a room with your dog. Call ahead for reservations and be sure to tell them that you are traveling with your dog. Ask about the hotel's dog policy. It is often disappointing, but it is much better to know in advance than to find out once you arrive. You have a much better chance of being allowed to stay if you have a wire dog crate with you. Some hotels may require a deposit.

# Nineteen

# *To Board or Not to Board, That Is the Question*

**B**oarding a dog is much harder on the person leaving him there than it is on the dog. Experienced kennel managers leave boxes of Kleenex all over the place for tearful farewells from guilt-ridden pet owners. But animals are not unhappy about a stay at a good kennel because they enjoy the company of other dogs. This will surprise some people and it may even disappoint others. Deep down, we want our dogs to miss us terribly and jump for joy when we return. You can start boarding your dog as young as six months. This makes boarding easier on you and the dog. With few exceptions, dogs adjust quickly to a kennel, and then begin to thrive. This is true, of course, provided the kennel personnel understand animals and are kind and attentive.

The traditional boarding kennel has indoor/outdoor dog runs with only one dog in each run. These are ideal for dogs. Some boarding kennels have indoor facilities only and may refer to themselves as "luxury" pet hotels. They provide a primary sleeping area for the dog and a door leading to an exercise run, all indoors. This can be a good situation for some dogs, especially those that shiver in the winter and overheat in the summer. Air conditioning and proper heating make this arrangement adequate all year round. To board or not to board is not a difficult question if you take the time to gather information from reliable sources. Talk to a vet or someone who has boarded his dog and knows about what is available in your area.

### Boarding your dog versus hiring a pet sitter

It is important to provide the best care when you are unable to be at home. There are advantages and disadvantages in each of these alternatives when leaving your dog behind. Only you can decide which is the best choice for you, your dog, and your situation.

### PET SITTER

| *Advantages* | *Problems* |
| --- | --- |
| • Your dog can stay in his own home, where everything is familiar. | • There is no one to care for your dog twenty-four hours a day, seven days a week. Once the pet sitter leaves, the |
| • If your dog has never been boarded away | |

from home, he will feel more comfortable in his own home and territory.

- Because he is not being exposed to other dogs, there is less opportunity for catching canine illnesses.

dog is on his own.

- If the dog becomes sick there is no veterinarian on call as there is in most boarding kennels. Unless the pet sitter is there, emergencies must wait.

- There is always the possibility of the dog escaping from the house or the yard.

- Pet sitters are often more expensive.

## BOARDING

### *Advantages*

- There is twenty-four-hour, seven-days-a-week supervision.
- A veterinarian is always on call.
- There are trained personnel on staff to care for your dog.
- Boarding kennels are always safe and secure. Your dog is protected at all times, and there is no opportunity for getting loose.
- Your dog will be so-

### *Problems*

- Your dog might become stressed if he has never been in a kennel environment before.
- While exposed to other dogs your dog may develop kennel cough, a highly contagious form of bronchitis characterized by a high-pitched cough. It is similar to sending your child to school, where there is always a chance of catching a cold from

cialized with new people and dogs. The added benefit here is that he will not be lonely.

another child.

- Without high-quality dog food and lack of exercise your dog may experience a loss of weight. This can also occur if the dog is emotionally stressed.

## BOARDING WITH A VETERINARIAN

### *Advantages*

- There will always be professional care available.
- Should your dog become sick, he will receive immediate veterinary care.
- The staff knows your dog, his personality, and his individual needs.
- You may just feel more secure knowing your dog is with your vet.

### *Problems*

- Your dog is around sick dogs.
- The runs are small.
- There are usually no indoor/outdoor runs.
- There is little or no opportunity for socialization.

*It is very important that you check to see if your vet's boarding facility offers twenty-four-hour, seven-days-a-week supervision. Your dog should never be left alone all night in a cage that is unsupervised.*

## *Your dog becomes angry when left in a kennel*

People get angry. Dogs do not. Few dogs dislike a kennel, and they do not have a true sense of time as we understand it. They are just as happy to see you whether you have been gone for one hour or three days. You will get the same excited, happy greeting no matter when you return. If he was angry, he would ignore you and walk away. That never happens.

Millions of dog owners board their dogs in kennels each year. If all the dogs forgot their owners, there would be no boarding. This is not a problem. Your dog will never forget you and will always love you. Dogs are very forgiving. They never dwell in the past unless you have been abusive.

## *Your dog seems to have separation anxiety*

If your dog has never been left alone, he may develop this condition when being left alone for the first time. Separation anxiety is an extreme emotional state that some dogs experience when left alone. It results in anxiety and frustration for the dog, which usually triggers chewing and excess barking and is very often accompanied with intense escape behavior. Dog owners can add to the intensity of the dog's emotional state without even knowing it. Making too big a fuss when leaving the house seems to aggravate matters. In an attempt to avoid upsetting the dog, some people become overly exuberant, loving, and affectionate just before leaving. The silence afterward leaves the dog in an

emotional vacuum, which then creates the extreme reaction. It is important to understand that this lack of
experience in being alone creates an unhealthy frame
of mind for the dog, and when you put him in a boarding kennel for the first time he may become so
stressed he will go into culture shock. To avoid this,
begin boarding your dog at six months of age for short
stays. If you begin to feel anxious or guilty about it, try
to think of it as something similar to sending a child to
school for the first time. The boarding kennel can be a
very positive experience for you and your dog. He can
learn to adjust beautifully to being without his family
and you can overcome your feeling that he can't live
without you.

### *Weight loss can be normal for a dog being boarded*

Weight loss depends on the boarding history of your
dog and length of time you are leaving him for. For a
first-timer, there may be some weight loss due to the
emotional stress created by being in a strange environment. Active dogs may lose weight because they will
be getting more exercise. Some dogs may experience a
slight loss in weight if they are used to rich treats at
home. At a boarding kennel they will be on a very
healthy diet without "people" food.

### *What is kennel cough?*

Kennel cough is a highly contagious disease affect-
ing the respiratory system of dogs. The major sign of
kennel cough is a dry, hacking cough that is easily in-

duced. For example, simply walking the dog on a leash may cause a sudden fit of coughing. Owners may suspect that the dog has something caught in its throat or that it is trying to vomit. Observe your dog carefully so that you can report this to the veterinarian. Most cases of kennel cough will resolve in ten days to three weeks, but owners can make their dogs more comfortable by minimizing the coughing with a cough suppressant obtained from your veterinarian. The term "kennel cough" implies that this ailment can only be contracted at a kennel. This is not the case. Your dog can catch kennel cough any place where there are dogs. He can catch it from exposure to just a single infected dog that he comes in contact with. This can happen at a kennel, a grooming salon, a dog show, or at a veterinarian's clinic. Before boarding your dog, you should have him vaccinated against kennel cough by your veterinarian. If your dog has kennel cough, he should be isolated from other dogs so that it cannot transmit the disease to healthy ones, and then he should receive veterinary treatment.

# Twenty

# He's Driving
# Me Crazy
## (Behavior Problems)

*T*alk about the need for solutions, here is a broad category that can drive a dog owner to the not-so-funny farm. If your dog begs, borrows, or steals, it's no joke. Neither is barking to beat the band or chasing cars, and let's not even mention the "c" word. On second thought, we should mention it. One of the greatest problems all dog owners face sooner or later is *chewing!* If you have been there, then you know how costly and aggravating it can be. The c word can cost you the price of a new sofa or other items of furniture, and maybe a new wardrobe or two. Well, hang in there, dog persons, there are solutions to all these troubling behaviors. In this section we will zero in on most of those specific nuisances that lead to trouble for the dog and his family. To find the answers just check out the problem, listed in alphabetical order.

### Barking

YOUR DOG BARKS AT THE DELIVERY TRUCK, AND WHEN YOU TELL HIM "IT'S OKAY," TO CONSOLE HIM, IT ONLY MAKES MATTERS WORSE

The sounds of trucks may bother his hearing. A dog's hearing can be five times more sensitive than human hearing. In this situation many dog owners say, "Okay," in order to quiet the dog. Unfortunately, this gives him a mixed message. When you do that you are actually telling him to bark because a soothing "okay" is a reward for whatever he is doing. If you want to stop him from barking at a truck or car you must correct the dog and *then* reward him with verbal praise. Use the corrective jerk, and a verbal correction "no." See the section on lease correction in Chapter 4, "He Won't Listen to Me." Another technique is the use of a spray bottle. You simply squirt the dog with room-temperature water when he barks. You also can take an empty soda can and fill it with twenty pennies, tape the opening, then shake it behind your back. Say "no" in a firm tone of voice as you shake the can. It is essential that you praise your dog immediately after he responds to a correction. Your praise is his reward for obeying.

YOUR DOG SITS BY THE WINDOW AND BARKS AT ANYONE WHO WALKS IN FRONT OF YOUR HOUSE WHEN YOU'RE NOT HOME

If you have drapes, curtains, or window shades, close them. Try confining your dog to a different area of the house. If this does not work, then place the training collar and leash on the dog ten minutes before you go out. Pretend to leave and actually close the door. Walk away. Quietly return undetected. Wait until he begins the full cycle of barking and go back into the house quickly. Take a hold of the leash and administer a leash correction with a firm, loud "no." Wait about five seconds and praise the dog for obeying your correction. The praise is essential. Repeat this technique as often as necessary until this behavior is changed. Do not expect perfection.

### YOUR DOG BARKS EXCESSIVELY WHEN YOU LEAVE HIM ALONE

He may be improperly confined—for example, kept behind a closed door, tied up—or he may be reacting to being left alone for the first time. If the issue is separation anxiety, make sure that he is properly confined when you are home so that he gets used to being by himself even though you are home. Use a puppy gate so that he can still see out, even though he is confined and left alone. Never tie up or chain your dog; it only worsens the condition.

### YOUR DOG BARKS AT OTHER DOGS THAT APPROACH HIM

Giving your dog basic obedience training is a must for this problem. Concentrate on the stationary commands such as sit, down, and stay. It is hard for a dog to bark when he is not moving. This will also give you much more control over the dog's behavior, so that when he barks you only have to say "no" to get him to stop.

## YOUR PUPPY BARKS ALL NIGHT LONG IN HIS CRATE

Make sure you have the right type of crate. It should be made of thin wires so that he can see out. Do not use a solid crate meant for shipping purposes; it is dark inside and too confining. If your puppy recently left his first home and his litter mates and mother, you can be sure he is lonesome and frightened. Have something warm and comfortable in his crate with him, such as a soft, rolled-up towel, a hot-water bottle (wrapped in a towel), or some of his favorite toys, so it will feel like his home. It would be nice to have something in the crate that still had the scent of his former home on it. Of course, he may be telling you that he's hungry or that he has to do his business.

## YOUR DOG BARKS EVERY TIME THE DOORBELL OR PHONE RINGS

Dogs' hearing is very sensitive. Certain sounds upset them. A good solution would be to toss him the ball or toy to distract him every time the bell or phone rings. It may also create a pleasant association with the ringing bell. Think Pavlov. Barking is okay; excessive barking is not.

## YOUR DOG BARKS LOUDLY. YOU WOULD LIKE HIM TO BARK SOFTER

The only solution here is to put cotton in your ears.

## YOUR DOG BARKS EVERY TIME YOU TIE HIM UP IN THE YARD. YOU WOULD LIKE TO MAKE HIM STOP

First of all, you should never tie up your dog. Dogs become more territorial when they are confined, and tying them up brings out their protective instinct, which almost always inspires barking. Construct a dog run or fence in your backyard so that he can be confined without being tied up or chained. When all else fails, use a leash correction accompanied with the verbal correction "no." (See the section on lease correction in Chapter 4, "He Won't Listen to Me.") Another technique is the use of a spray bottle. You simply squirt the dog with room-temperature water when he barks. You also can take an empty soda can and fill it with twenty pennies, tape the opening, then shake it behind your back. Say "no" in a firm tone of voice as you shake the can. It is essential that you praise your dog immediately after he responds to a correction.

### YOUR DOG BARKS AND LUNGES AT THE BACKYARD FENCE WHENEVER SOMEONE WALKS BY. YOU'D LIKE TO STOP THIS

Use the leash correction accompanied with the verbal correction "no." (See the section on lease correction in Chapter 4, "He Won't Listen to Me.") It is essential that you praise your dog immediately after he responds to a correction.

Once that works, get a thirty-foot leash, or a length of rope attached to your leash, so that you can correct him from a further distance. Or have somebody outside with a garden hose, and when he starts to bark or lunge, have that person squirt him as you say "no" in a loud, firm tone of voice. After that, you can give him a bath.

### Begging

YOUR DOG BEGS FOR PEOPLE FOOD AT THE TABLE. YOU
WANT THIS TO STOP

The simple answer is to stop feeding him from the table. Of course, people food seems appealing to the dog because of the cooking aromas and because he will always want what you are having. Most of the time it's a people problem. Stop spoiling your dog and learn to say "no."

There are three simple solutions. First, never feed him from the table. Second, teach him the command "place" (see the section on place in Chapter 4, "He Won't Listen to Me."). This is a training command that gets the dog to remain in one place while you have dinner in another place. He remains there until you are finished. Last, employ the command down/stay outside the room. Any of these solutions will work and make everybody happy, especially your dinner guests.

YOUR DOG BEGS FOR FOOD AT THE TABLE AND YOU FEAR
IT MAY BE BECAUSE YOU DON'T FEED HIM ENOUGH

Dogs beg constantly for food at the table because their families indulge it. In the beginning it is fun and heartwarming. It soon becomes an annoying habit that you are stuck with. If you are feeding your dog a proper diet of dog food, he is not begging because he is not being fed enough.

WHEN I PUT TABLE SCRAPS IN MY DOG'S FOOD, HE THEN
BEGS AT THE TABLE

Your dog is pretty smart. He knows exactly when his next meal is coming because you always give him table scraps. The problem of begging at the table will stop when you stop feeding the dog table scraps.

### Biting

#### DOES ONE DOG BREED BITE MORE THAN OTHERS?

No, that is a false impression. Some of the breeds that get bad press are Rottweilers, Pit Bulls, German Shepherd Dogs, and Doberman Pinschers. As specific breeds become popular, the desire for them increases in great numbers and the demand far outweighs the supply. The result is a tremendous amount of nonselective, indiscriminate commercial breeding of every dog that can breathe no matter what its medical or behavioral history. Sometimes certain natural tendencies, such as aggressiveness, become more pronounced because of this kind of breeding. Dogs that are shy, dogs that have hip dysplasia, dogs with asthma, dogs that bite, dogs that are frightened, dogs that are ferocious—all are bred without any thought or consideration for these very important factors inherited from their parents or grandparents. This is the cause of many dog bites.

The popularity of certain breeds stems from television, movies, advertising, or those that are owned by the rich and famous. When the president of the United States acquired a chocolate-colored Labrador Retriever the demand for that breed increased a thousand times. Many of the larger breeds are desired because of their protection value as well as the companionship they offer. If you consider dog-bite statistics in the United States, you will discover there are four million dog bites reported each year and an estimated four million unreported, 95 percent of which are caused by a family or neighborhood pet. Of those dogs that have bitten there is a listing of eighty to a hundred different breeds represented. Unfortunately, there is a disproportionate focus on a few of the large, notorious breeds, because they are capable of doing the most physical damage. Although few small dog breeds can actually kill somebody, the medical harm they can bring to children can be catastrophic. Yes, even small dogs can and do bite, causing pain and suffering.

## WHY DO DOGS BITE?

Certain dogs that are bred indiscriminately and sold commercially in great quantities often wind up with a greater genetic predisposition for aggressive behavior. Generally, dogs bite because they are often bred indiscriminately without regard for this predisposition. Such dogs are produced in great quantities and sold commercially in some pet shops and kennels. Dogs also bite because of their lack of interaction with other dogs and people, or because of poor living conditions, cruel and abusive treatment from uneducated or unkind owners, or from improper handling and rearing.

## TRAINING A DOG NOT TO BITE

It can be done. It involves controlling your dog's behavior through obedience training and reconditioning. Training and handling a dangerous dog or one that has already bitten someone is risky and unsafe for typical dog owners. It requires knowledge and experience. It is best to seek help from a professional dog trainer or animal behaviorist.

### WHEN YOUR DOG IS GOING TO BITE

There are warning signs that your dog is about to bite you or someone near him. As a responsible dog owner you must become aware of these warning signs. If your dog barks aggressively, lunges at people, or behaves in a fearful manner but still barks and growls it is quite likely that the next step will be to bite. The most misunderstood warning sign of all is the growl. When a dog growls from deep within his throat it should be taken as a serious threat that is meant to warn you about an impending bite.

### YOUR DOG DOESN'T LIKE OTHER DOGS

Your dog may not like other dogs and you have to accept that fact. What you can do to control his aggressive behavior is to use reconditioning techniques such as the leash correction to stop his behavior with a firm "no." You should also have your dog fully trained so that his desire to please you is greater than his aggressiveness toward other dogs. Group training socializes your dog to be more tolerant and is a good option once your dog is six months old.

### AFTER GROWING UP TOGETHER AND LIVING PEACEABLY FOR A LONG TIME, YOUR TWO DOGS NO LONGER GET ALONG AND INEXPLICABLY ATTACK EACH OTHER

One of the myths of owning two dogs is that they will love each other for life and never fight, especially if they are of the same sex and have been raised together. Dogs of the same sex have issues over territory, food, toys, and their owners. These problems usually begin after the first year together. The key to successfully living with dogs of the same sex is to avoid situations where they may become aggressive. For example, feed them separately and give them their own toys and living spaces (separate crates). Give deference to whichever one is the dominant dog. That's the one who must get first consideration in all matters. Obedience training for both dogs is a must. In some cases you may have to get rid of one of the dogs; it depends on how aggressive the dogs are.

### YOUR DOG DOESN'T LIKE YOUR VET. HE GROWLS AND TRIES TO BITE HIM WHEN HE IS EXAMINED

One solution is to examine your dog yourself every day to get him used to being touched. Reward him with lavish praise each time you do this as well as with an assortment of food treats he likes. If you do this every day he will look forward to his examinations with you and with the vet.

### YOU ARE EXPECTING A CHILD AND YOUR DOG HAS NEVER BEEN AROUND CHILDREN

If you are a new puppy owner and you want your dog to be good with kids, he must be socialized with children as much as possible so he is comfortable around them. All dogs should be socialized with children so that when a baby comes into the family, he feels comfortable with and accepting of the new family member. If you have a mature dog that has never lived with a child, there is no guarantee that he will adjust to the new baby. This means you must take certain precautions. It is essential that you never leave your dog alone with a baby or young child. Never allow a child to grab hold of the dog; dogs will bite when they are being hurt or if they think they are being attacked.

### WHEN SOMEONE APPROACHES THE DOOR, YOUR DOG SNARLS, GROWLS, AND BARES HIS TEETH. HE LOOKS LIKE HE WILL BITE

Dogs are very territorial in nature and believe they are protecting their homes or their owners. Some people like this defensiveness because they think their dogs are being protective when, in fact, they are being too aggressive. You must correct this type of behavior with a firm leash correction.

### YOUR DOG SEEMS TO LIKE ONLY CERTAIN PEOPLE

Not all dogs like all people. For example, when they have been raised exclusively with women, they may not like men. The opposite of this may also apply. There are dogs who have been raised exclusively with other dogs for the first year of their lives and consequently are not very friendly with people. Some dog owners keep their dogs away from strangers so they can be protective. This tactic results in encouraging dogs to be shy or aggressive and thus not very good with people outside their own families.

Most likely, your dog was not socialized properly. He may not have been around different people or exposed to a wide variety of humans on a regular basis. Exposing him to the outside world, taking him for extensive walks, and using positive reconditioning techniques such as verbal praise or food rewards when he meets new people will make him a more trusting and confident dog.

### YOUR PUPPY SEEMS TO BITE ALL THE TIME

All puppies teethe from the age of five weeks to six months. They are in pain as they replace their baby teeth with their permanent ones. Ice cubes can be very soothing for their sore gums. Give them a few whenever they seem to be chewing excessively. Another gum soother is a frozen washcloth. Soak six washcloths in cold water, twist them into ropes, and put them in the freezer. Give your puppy a frozen washcloth every two hours to chew on. The coldness will numb the gums and ease the pain.

### YOUR DOG BITES CHILDREN MORE THAN ADULTS

Children tend to play rough with dogs and do not realize that they may be hurting or scaring their pets. This is more likely to happen if the children have no experience with dogs or have never been around them. It really doesn't matter to the dog if he has been hurt accidentally or on purpose. Bear in mind that dogs naturally expect a social order in their packs or families. If yours is the top dog and is aggressive in nature, he will not tolerate too much from little people. Statistics show that boys get bitten twice as often as girls, presumably because they play rougher.

### Your dog is properly trained for protection work so he is not dangerous to people

If a dog is professionally trained for protection work, he is supposed to be well socialized with all types of people. He must also be extremely obedient so that he can respond instantly to his owner's commands and therefore be under control at all times. Properly trained protection dogs may be the safest dogs to own.

## Car behavior

### You want to introduce your dog to riding in a car

The younger your dog is the better. Expose him to the experience of riding as soon as possible, because the sooner you do it the more comfortable he will be as an adult. Riding in a car should be a pleasant experience for a dog.

### Your dog rides in the car and sticks his head out the window

Your dog should never be allowed to stick his head out the car window when riding in your car. The wind and dust will irritate his eyes. He could jump out of the window and get seriously injured or killed.

### You can't control your dog when he becomes wild in the car

Three simple solutions: First, use a doggie seat belt. Second, have him ride in a wire dog crate. Three, have your dog trained. This is a necessity in all circumstances. The most useful training commands for this purpose are "down" and "stay."

### YOU LIKE TO LET YOUR DOG RIDE IN YOUR LAP

Do not do it. This could cause serious accidents for both you and your pet because he is likely to block your vision while driving. If you get into an accident or stop suddenly, the dog could be thrown from the vehicle or he could fall or jump to the floor and prevent you from using your gas or brake pedal. The best solution here is to use a doggie seat belt or wire dog crate.

### YOU LET YOUR DOG RIDE IN THE BACK OF A PICKUP TRUCK

No dog should ever be allowed to ride in the back of an open pickup truck. He could jump out and get hit by a car. Riding in an open truck also could bring about sunstroke or promote physical injury of all sorts. It is irresponsible dog ownership to permit this.

### YOUR DOG ALWAYS GETS SICK WHEN HE RIDES IN A CAR

Dogs experience motion sickness as a result of abrupt starts and stops or from the constant swinging motion of the car. Other causes may be engine fumes, lack of ventilation, temperatures that are either too hot or too cold, or in some rare instances from a medical problem. Most dogs stand as they ride in the car, but if the car is moving too fast or your driving is erratic, you are probably causing the problem. The answer could be a few brush-up driving lessons. If the dog is new to riding in the car his problem may be an emotional one. The dog may be reacting to the newness of the experience or perhaps responding to a negative association such as being hurt while in the car.

Just as some humans get sick from curvy roads, so do some dogs. It is probably the result of the extreme turns causing the car to swerve from side to side. As the car veers, so does the dog, upsetting his stomach. As the dog peers out the window he can see how high he is, and like many humans becomes frightened and then sick to his stomach. At that point he may feel he would rather have stayed home.

Your dog will not avoid car sickness by riding on a full stomach. On the contrary, you should feed your dog six to eight hours before taking him out for a long drive. If you feed him right away, it is highly likely that he will vomit in the car. He also may develop diarrhea. Always bring plastic bags and paper towels and odor neutralizer with you when taking the dog out in the car. You never know when you will need them.

Make the riding experience a pleasant one by talking to your dog in a happy, soothing tone of voice. Praise him and tell him what a good dog he is for riding so well. Give him some toys to play with and something to chew on. Keep him secure by placing him in a wire dog crate or hooked into a seat belt designed for dogs. Start riding in the car with him at a young age so that he is well adjusted by the time he is an adult dog.

## YOUR DOG BECOMES FRIGHTENED WHENEVER YOU PUT HIM IN THE CAR

Some dogs do not love riding in the car. It may be a terrifying experience, especially if he is not properly secured. Imagine how he must feel when you make sharp turns and sudden stops. The dog loses his ability to stand and tumbles back and forth. It probably feels like he's in an accident. Make sure your dog is secured properly. If you stabilize him with a doggie seat belt or place him in a wire dog crate, eventually he will become less frightened of being in the car. We also recommend that as many trips in the car as possible should be to pleasant places such as the park, the beach, friends' homes, or even shopping. For many dogs the only time they ride in the car is to the vet's office, the groomer, or to a boarding kennel.

## Car chasing

### YOUR DOG LIKES TO CHASE CARS

Chasing cars involves two instincts. The first is the need to defend territory and to attack or drive off any intruder in that territory. The second involves a strong hunting instinct with an intense prey drive. Imagine your dog living in the wild and having to depend on hunting to survive. If something moves quickly, he would chase after it almost immediately. He would survive only by chasing after a prey animal, capturing it, and then killing it. It would be the only way he could have food. When your dog chases cars, he is acting on one or the other of these instincts.

### YOU CAN'T GET YOUR DOG TO STOP CHASING CARS

On-leash obedience training is an absolute necessity. When your dog starts chasing a car, you need to give him a command such as "sit" or "down." If that doesn't work, try executing a very strong leash correction, as you say, "no," in a loud, firm tone of voice. Immediately following the leash correction you must command the dog into a sit or down position. Once you've accomplished this procedure with a six-foot leash, graduate to a thirty-foot leash so he can be corrected from greater distances, applying the same techniques as with the six-foot leash. One of the most successful training techniques for this problem is to teach your dog boundaries. Never walk your dog in the street—never let him leave the curb—without the release command "okay." Make sure the dog stays in place until you give him the release command to move when opening the front door or gate.

Obedience training is the most effective and simple way to make sure your dog never chases cars. Make sure he gets lots of exercise and is confined properly. Make sure your fences are at least six- to eight-feet high and use self-locking gates. Effective prevention can be as easy as remembering to close the gate at all times. Prevention techniques save lives.

### Chewing

You've let your puppy out of his crate and now he's chewing everything

This is a bad idea. Your expectations are greater than your dog's ability to control himself, especially if he has a chewing problem. Here is the rule: A dog should be two years or older to have complete run of the house, whether he is a chewer or not. That is when most dogs mature. Do not be fooled by the size of your dog. Your one-year-old dog could weigh ninety pounds but is still a puppy in every way.

It is wrong to think that he is ready for the big world since he was "so wonderful and well trained" in the crate. Regardless of size, puppies usually do not mature until the age of two. Until then they must be confined when no one is home. If you feel that your dog has outgrown his crate, try the following solutions. Confine him in an area of the house that has a tile or linoleum floor, such as the bathroom or the kitchen. Keep him behind a baby gate so that he can see out without feeling too restricted. Use your yard if it is fenced in or build a dog run, which is an excellent alternative.

There are other reasons for chewing besides youthful misbehaving. For example, puppies from five to six months of age have teething pain, as new teeth erupt through the gums, just like human babies. Give teething puppies a dish of ice cubes to chew on. The cold will ease the soreness of the gums. Take six wash cloths and soak them in cold water. Pull them into long ropes and twist them. Place them in the freezer and give a new one to your puppy every two hours. The coldness will numb his gums and ease the pain.

### YOUR PUPPY PUSHES OUT THE BOTTOM TRAY OF HIS DOG CRATE AND CHEWS ON THE CARPET WHEN YOU LEAVE HOME

He does not do this because he doesn't like the crate or because he is lonely. He may be confined in the crate for too long a period of time or perhaps he has a high-energy personality. If so, he will need a lot more exercise. Give him a variety of toys to keep him occupied, especially chew toys. Make sure he is in a wire dog crate where he can see out, rather than in an airline shipping crate with solid walls. Get a marrow bone from the butcher, stuff it with peanut butter, cheese, or bologna, and he will spend hours trying to lick it out. The idea is to redirect his chewing to something acceptable, such as the marrow bone, or to help the dog use up his excess energy.

### YOUR MATURE DOG STILL CHEWS DESTRUCTIVELY IF LEFT ALONE FOR MORE THAN AN HOUR

There are a number of reasons for this behavior. The dog may suffer with separation anxiety, which involves fear and panic whenever the owner leaves the dog alone. This creates uncontrollable chewing behavior with anything he can sink his teeth into. It can be an attempt to chew through the wall to escape or simply an expression of nervous energy created by the emotions. One practical solution is to give the dog vigorous exercise before leaving him alone. If the dog has too much freedom when you leave, you cannot predict what he is going to chew next. Therefore, you must confine him behind a baby gate in an area such as the kitchen. By confining the dog, you can set him up in a situation where you can correct his behavior. For example, make available something that he shouldn't chew. Purchase alum powder, a bitter, pungent seasoning, in a pharmacy, add water, and make a thick paste. Smear it on the object that you do not want him to chew and, for good measure, place a dab on the dog's tongue. The alum paste tastes bad and also has a puckering effect on the mouth. It is unpleasant. This will effectively stop the dog from chewing whatever had the alum paste on it. At the same time leave the dog's favorite toy in the same room so that he has an alternative to chewing up your home.

## YOUR DOG CHEWS WHEN HE'S HUNGRY OR BORED

Some dogs chew because they are hungry and not being fed enough food. Some dogs are not being fed balanced diets, which could also create a chewing problem. Consult a veterinarian for advice about your dog's proper diet. It may help. Boredom is another important reason for destructive chewing. Some dogs require more exercise than others, such as those of the hunting breeds, the hound breeds, the terriers, and a number of the working breeds. Vigorous exercise and play sessions can be an important solution for this problem. Do not allow your dog to become a couch potato. You must make the effort to exercise with your dog. It will be good for both of you. Obedience training offers many opportunities to alleviate boredom and, as a bonus, resolve chewing problems. It will be fun to teach your dog to retrieve or to participate in agility exercises. Develop games and activities with your dog on a daily basis, such as having a Frisbee toss (make sure he isn't allowed to chew it).

## YOUR DOG HAS EATEN YOUR NEW SOFA AND YOU ARE BEING PRESSURED BY YOUR HUSBAND TO GET RID OF HIM

This is a people problem as well as a dog problem. It is common for dogs that are allowed to sleep in your bed also to sleep on your sofa. If you allow your dog to sleep on the bed, then he probably considers the sofa to be just another bed. This sets the scene for destructive chewing. By allowing your dog on one piece of furniture, you are allowing him to be on all the furniture; they cannot make the distinction between pieces of furniture. The first part of the solution is to give the dog his own bed, either a wire dog crate, a commercial dog bed, or the floor with a pillow or blanket. The next part is to stop allowing the dog to sleep on the furniture, including your bed. Most chewing problems occur when you are not home. Here are some practical solutions: Lay a piece of chicken wire over the furniture you do not want the dog to sleep on; very few dogs will want to sleep on that. You may get the same result with long sheets of aluminum foil. The dog will not like the feel or the sound of it and is very likely to stay away from it. Or put baking trays on the sofa; they will be uncomfortable to lay on.

### YOUR DOG CHEWS YOUR POSSESSIONS IN FRONT OF YOU EVEN AFTER YOU YELL "NO"

Even when you yell at your dog he stops his chewing only for a short time, then returns to finish the job. The most effective solution for this problem is to employ a leash correction, which is sometimes referred to as the corrective jerk. Place the leash and collar on the dog, and allow him to walk around the house with them dangling from his neck. (You must use this technique at a time that you can stay home.) Every time you see him begin to chew on one of your possessions, give him a leash correction. Hold the leash with both hands a bit below waist level. Jerk the leash sideways and slightly upward to the right. As you jerk the leash, say "no" in a firm tone of voice. Return to the original position in one quick motion. Adjust the strength of your correction to the size and personality of your dog. As soon as he stops his behavior, lavish him with praise and affection.

The verbal and physical correction given at the same time makes a lasting impression on the dog and eventually trains him to stop this unwanted behavior. The biggest mistake that dog owners can make is to give the dog too much freedom. If you want to stop your dog's chewing problem permanently and prevent destruction of your possessions, leave the leash and collar on the dog while you are home. Whenever he begins to chew, give him a firm correction. You will be amazed how quickly the chewing problem will go away.

## Coprophagy (stool eating)
### YOUR DOG EATS HIS OWN STOOL

Dogs engage in this seemingly strange behavior for a number of reasons. There are always some unabsorbed nutrients and digestive enzymes in a dog's stool, making them adequate for recycling from the dog's point of view. Stool eating can be a source of food for a dog that eats too quickly and doesn't digest his food properly. A dog suffering from parasites may engage in this behavior. Stool eating may be a reaction to negative treatment from the dog's family, when the dog is punished for housebreaking accidents. If the owner pushes the dog's face in his own mess, he may attempt to eat the evidence. Poor hygiene is yet one other cause. It is important to clean up after your dog immediately. Some of the hunting breeds instinctively carry objects in their mouths, such as dead birds and other prey animals. If they do not have this opportunity, they just might use their stool to satisfy the instinct.

Coprophagy can be a response to negative emotions, such as loneliness or fear or even boredom. Solutions to these problems seem self-evident. Environmental solutions for this problem involve cleaning up after the dog as soon as possible and to housebreak instead of paper train so there is no opportunity for this habit to get started. Try introducing an additive to the dog's food that will make the stool extremely unpleasant, such as meat tenderizers, sauerkraut, oil of anise, or a product called Forbid. Of course, the cure may be even less appealing than the problem. Before introducing an additive, please ask your veterinarian if this is the proper solution for your dog.

### WHEN YOU WALK YOUR DOG HE CONTINUALLY SNIFFS THE STOOLS OF OTHER DOGS AND SOMETIMES TRIES TO EAT THEM

This is not only an unpleasant habit, it can be medically harmful. Dog stools can be carriers of contagious diseases such as parvovirus and various parasites such as roundworms and tapeworms. Some of these can be contagious to humans. Give the dog a strong voice and leash correction whenever he engages in this practice.

### Digging

YOUR DOG LOVES TO DIG. HERE'S WHY

It is natural behavior for dogs to dig. When the weather is hot, they dig to cool off. When the weather is cold, they dig to make a warm place to bed down, outdoors. When living wild, dogs or wolves dig a hole and bury their food to hide it from marauders. When a dog destroys your yard by digging holes, it doesn't seem unreasonable to him. He cannot help himself. It is his birthright to dig.

YOU USE DOG STOOLS IN DUG-UP HOLES AS A PREVENTATIVE FOR DIGGING

Forget about it. This idea stinks. Dogs love their own stools.

YOU CAN'T GET YOUR DOG TO STOP DIGGING

Here are a few quick solutions: Fill all the existing holes dug by the dog with rocks. Add just enough dirt to cover them up. The dog will try to redig the holes. When he does he will scratch his paws on the rocks and discover he cannot do it. The sensation of hitting the rocks with his paws is not only unpleasant, but extremely frustrating. This is a self-correcting technique that does not seem to involve you. You can do the same with chicken wire or blown-up balloons (the noise will startle him when they pop). Your dog may be digging holes because he is hot and is trying to create a cool place for himself. If you feel this is the situation, then get him a child's wading pool and fill it with cool water. Let him lie in the water and refresh himself. It may stop him from digging. Beating the heat also can be accomplished by getting him a doghouse of his own, with some of his favorite toys inside. The same is true of a fenced-in dog run.

### YOU'VE HEARD ABOUT FILLING THE DUG-UP HOLES WITH WATER AND PUTTING THE DOG'S HEAD IN THEM AS PUNISHMENT FOR DIGGING

Find the person who told you that and put *his* head in the hole. Why would you want to drown your best friend? Punishments do not teach a dog what he should or shouldn't do. Do not do this!

### SOME BREEDS SEEM TO DIG MORE THAN OTHERS

Most dogs will dig holes in your yard if given the opportunity. If you provide them with soft soil and leave them alone, you will almost certainly have holes in your yard. However, most of the terrier breeds are more likely to dig than others. They have been bred to hunt by chasing after their prey into their holes. Rabbits, gophers, field mice, rats, fox, and other prey animals "go to ground," and the terriers, being the great hunters that they are, follow in hot pursuit. To do this they must be good diggers. It is their instinct to dig that makes them such effective hunters. A number of other sporting breeds also know how to "go to ground" and are likely to dig up your yard if given the chance. It's a natural instinct. Can you dig it?

## *Dogfighting*

YOU HAVE TWO MALE DOGS FROM THE SAME LITTER LIV-
ING TOGETHER, AND THEY FIGHT OFTEN OVER TOYS AND
PERSONAL POSSESSIONS

This is not about sibling rivalry. This is about territorial dominance and possessive aggressiveness. Like
most animals, dogs do not have the human view of
what is fair and what is not. They do deal with the
rights of possession. Dogs are organized to live with a
sense of territory and a social order based on dominance and subordination. The only way to deal with
this kind of situation in the human environment is to
gain control over your dogs. To do this you must train
them and teach them the commands "place" and
"stay." It will also help to get separate wire dog crates
and give them their own toys in their own spaces. This
is your best chance to make both dogs happy.

YOUR DOGS ALWAYS FIGHT AT FEEDING TIME

Always feed these dogs separately. You're asking for
trouble if you feed them in the same room. Usually
one dog is going to finish faster than the other and
then think, *I want some of yours.* That's when the fight
begins. Dogs do not have sharing attitudes.

YOUR DOGS ARE FIGHTING AND YOU DON'T KNOW HOW
TO BREAK THEM UP

Dogfighting is a serious situation. Dogs and people
can get injured badly. Prevention is the best idea. If
you know your dog is aggressive toward other dogs,
avoid confrontations. When you see another male dog

approaching you, go across the street or walk in the opposite direction. In the event of a dogfight, here are some solutions. Dowse the dogs with a bucket of water. Dowse them with a garden hose. A powerful water nozzle is the most effective. Throw a blanket over both dogs; it will disorient them. Make a loud noise to get their attention. Bang two pots together. Do not grab your dog by the tail or by the collar. Do not grab either dog; he may think you are the other dog and bite you.

### YOUR DOGS LOOK LIKE THEY'RE ABOUT TO FIGHT

Look and listen for any growling, barking, or lunging at the other dog. Beware of direct eye contact between dogs. Look for the body language of canine aggression: erect ears, elevated or downward tail, raised hackles along the spine.

### YOU'VE GOTTEN A SECOND DOG AND WANT TO INTRODUCE HIM TO YOUR FIRST DOG IN THE FRIENDLIEST WAY

Always introduce a new dog on neutral territory, off your property. For example, take both dogs to a different street or to a park and let them meet there. Make sure they are both on leashes. If they are of the opposite sex, there will probably be no problem. Problems most often develop between dogs of the same sex, especially if they are both adults. Usually an older dog and a puppy will not fight. If your second dog is of the same sex and he is a puppy, you may have a problem when he reaches maturity, which can be in one or two years. Obedience training and intelligent handling techniques will prevent most dog aggression problems.

## YOUR DOGS FIGHT OVER MEMBERS OF THE FAMILY, AND IT SEEMS LIKE JEALOUSY

Dogs do not experience jealousy as people do. Dogs often become territorial or protective about one or more persons in the family, and that may seem like jealousy, but it isn't. Jealousy is a sophisticated human emotion. Sometimes this is a dog problem and sometimes it is a people problem. Beware of the areas and times that this situation occurs. For example, if your dog is on the bed with one member of the family and another person walks in, the dog may growl. This could happen in other areas of the house as well. When this happens you must take immediate corrective measures. Leash corrections are the best way to stop this behavior. You must not allow the dog to be the leader of the pack (or family). You must take charge.

## YOUR FEMALE DOG FIGHTS WITH OTHER FEMALES MORE OFTEN THAN MALES

Dogs of the same sex, whether they are males or females, fight with each other more than with those of the opposite sex. The issue is dominance, or who is the top dog. When confronted with this situation you must always favor the dominant dog. It may not sound fair, but it is the only practical solution in terms of natural dog behavior. Give the dominant dog love and attention first. Feed him first and make sure he has first privileges in all things. In a human family older brothers and sisters have seniority and therefore more privileges than younger brothers or sisters.

### YOUR DOG GETS AGGRESSIVE WITH OTHER DOGS IN HIS OWN TERRITORY, BUT LEAVES THEM ALONE IN A PARK

Most dogs are more territorial in their own environment, whether they're at home, in their yard, in the family car, or simply standing next to their owners. When they go to a dog park, it is neutral ground. There is no need to defend the territory because it isn't their own territory. Aggression will not occur, most of the time. But don't count on it. Some dogs will get aggressive at dog parks too if they are very dominant types.

### YOU ARE WORRIED THAT A DOMINANT DOG WILL NOT GET ALONG WITH A SUBORDINATE DOG IN THE SAME HOUSE

They will get along fine in most cases. One dog becomes the alpha dog, or top dog, and dominates the other dog. This is the ideal situation if you have more than one dog. Remember, always give the dominant dog first choice in all matters.

### YOUR DOG IS MORE AGGRESSIVE ON THE LEASH THAN OFF

Dogs are extremely territorial and you are a part of their territory, especially while the leash connects you to each other. You may think that you are holding your dog on leash. But from the dog's point of view, he is holding you on the leash and is protecting you. In other words, he is protecting what he believes is part of his territory. Off leash, you are on your own. It is interesting to note that many working breeds and most terriers are more protective or territorial than others. If your dog is too aggressive on the leash you must have him trained. Socializing your dog with other dogs and new people is another important solution.

## YOUR DOG FIGHTS WITH SOME DOGS AND NOT WITH OTHERS

If your dog is very dominant, he will feel challenged if he meets up with another dominant dog. In that situation they are going to try to establish which is the top dog. A barking, growling, snarling, and fighting match is likely to happen. This is more to be expected on your dog's own territory than at any other place. Being neutered helps dominant dogs become less dangerous, especially males. Female dogs are spayed and male dogs are castrated. This involves the surgical removal of the reproductive organs. In males it takes approximately six weeks for the hormone testosterone to leave the body. In that time his behavior will become less aggressive and less territorial.

### Excessive wetting

## YOUR DOG BECOMES NERVOUS AND WETS WHEN HE HEARS LOUD NOISES

Your dog may have a noise phobia and submissively wets whenever he is frightened by a strange or new sound. Never raise your voice to your dog and only use positive reconditioning solutions to help overcome the fear. One of the best solutions is to purchase a commercially produced audiotape of environmental sounds of things that frighten the dog, such as rain, surf, thunderstorms, auto traffic, even gunshots. Always start by playing the gentlest sounds. As you play the sound, reassure the dog with a gentle tone of voice. Keep playing each sound until the dog doesn't respond with fear. Once that happens, praise him and reward him with a small food treat in addition to loving affection. Continue the process to the next sound until he overcomes his fear of new sounds.

### YOUR PUPPY WETS ALL DAY LONG, AND YOU DON'T KNOW IF IT'S A TRAINING PROBLEM OR A MEDICAL PROBLEM

The first order of business is to ask your veterinarian about this. The dog could have a bladder infection or some other medical problem. It is important to rule this out. If your dog does not have a medical problem, the constant wetting could have something to do with age or size. It has to do with too much water and lack of bladder control. A toy breed such as a Maltese is likely to have less bladder control than one of the larger breeds such as Siberian Husky. Because you do not want to be cleaning urine off the floor all day you will need to set up an appropriate schedule for giving the dog water. Normal, healthy dogs do not need water all day, especially if they are in an air-conditioned home in the warm weather and if there is an adequate walking schedule. On the other hand, if your dog is kept outside, then it doesn't matter if he has water all day. It is then a matter of logic. When a human drinks eight to ten glasses of water all day, he or she is going to be in the bathroom a lot, wouldn't you think?

## WHEN YOU TRY PUTTING A LEASH AND COLLAR ON YOUR DOG HE WETS THE FLOOR

There are reasons and solutions for this problem. Some dogs get very excited about going outside. If that's the case, simply put the leash and collar on the dog outside. Perhaps he's had too much water. If so, give him water every three or four hours, rather than all day long. If he seems frightened of the leash and collar or of your body language when reaching down, spend some time making the leash and collar a fun thing. Make a game out of it and give the dog lavish verbal praise. Try to make it all seem like fun. Oh, yes. Make sure the dog is on a linoleum surface when you place the leash and collar on him. That will at least save your carpet.

## WHEN YOU YELL AT YOUR DOG, HE WETS

Stop yelling at him. A dog's hearing is at least five times better than ours and makes them more sensitive to loud noises. You may be scaring your dog by being too loud, which would cause him to wet the floor.

## WHEN YOU COME HOME, YOUR DOG GETS SO EXCITED, HE PEES ALL OVER THE FLOOR

This is not a housebreaking problem, it is an excitement problem. When you enter the house, try not to excite your dog with too much enthusiasm. Until the dog becomes more mature, make your arrival more subdued, with as little fuss as possible. Greet your dog, of course, but do not make it seem like you haven't been together for weeks. Bear in mind that some young dogs do not have the same bladder control as mature dogs. If such a dog drinks too much water and becomes overly excited he is going to lose it, all over the floor. Give him water every three or four hours only. Teach your dog the command "sit." When you get home, give him that command so he has something he must do, rather than wiggle all over. Then place him in "stay." If this is just a puppy problem, have him greet you outside . . . and wear old shoes.

### You've noticed that some breeds of dogs have more wetting problems than others

This may not be a breed problem. It usually has to do with the age of the dog, his water intake, and his personality type. For example, an excitable, nervous, or fearful type dog is likely to have a wetting problem. Smaller dogs have smaller bladders, which can also cause the problem.

### Your dog wets only when he seems frightened

Shy dogs lose bladder control if they are yelled at or treated harshly in any way. Be aware of your body language. You may be intimidating your dog by hovering over him or moving in a threatening manner, from his point of view. Never hit, yell, or point your finger at your dog in an intimidating way. You can overcome your dog's fear and eliminate this problem completely by openly expressing your love for him and by training him with positive reinforcements such as lavish praise for doing a good job.

### *Fear of confinement*

WHEN YOU PUT YOUR DOG IN THE CRATE, HE HOWLS
AND CRIES UNTIL YOU CAN'T STAND IT, AND THEN YOU
LET HIM OUT. IT MAKES YOU FEEL SO MEAN

Your dog is obviously not used to being confined in
a crate. Dogs need to be taught how to make themselves comfortable and how to feel better. One way to
deal with this problem is to feed your dog in his crate.
Try putting his toys in the crate along with a soft towel
or blanket just to make it feel more homelike. Also,
leave the door open when you're home so that he
doesn't feel trapped. Going in the crate then becomes
his choice, because he can walk out anytime, as long
as you are there. Always use a wire crate so he can see
out. The airline or travel crates that are perfect for
traveling are not necessarily appropriate for the home,
because there is only a small window on the side and a
front gate. This is what makes your dog feel trapped.

YOUR PUPPY IS AFRAID TO GO IN THE BATHROOM WHERE
YOU CONFINE HIM DURING THE DAY. WHEN YOU CLOSE
THE DOOR, HE SCRATCHES AND CRIES LIKE HE IS BEING
PUNISHED

You are scaring your dog. He feels frightened and
abandoned when you confine him behind a closed
door. Use a puppy gate or a child's gate instead of the
closed door to confine him, so he can see out. These
are available in a hardware store or in a pet supplies
outlet. Keep the lights on when you go and give him
some of his favorite toys. Leave a radio playing with
soothing music. You should consider a larger area for

confinement, such as the kitchen, where he is probably fed. That is bound to be more comfortable for him.

YOUR DOG HOWLS EVERY TIME YOU CLOSE HIM IN THE
GARAGE. YOU LEAVE A LIGHT ON AND HE HAS A BED IN
THERE BUT HE STILL HOWLS

A garage is not likely to be a warm and inviting place for a dog to be confined. As a matter of fact, it is a pretty grim place to be confined. If your garage is like most others, it is uncomfortable, unheated, without air conditioning, and, of course, without windows. Find a nice homey environment such as your kitchen, or, if you have one, an outside area, where you can install a dog run. Garages are for cars and tools, not dogs.

YOU'RE NOT SURE YOUR DOG IS READY TO HAVE THE RUN
OF THE ENTIRE HOUSE WITHOUT BEING CONFINED

Most dogs take at least two years and even longer before they are truly matured. If your dog has been trained, take it one room at a time and then expand his freedom every few days. See how he handles this. Dogs need to feel secure. Too much freedom all at once can be overwhelming and get them in trouble. It's the same as raising children.

### Fear of noises

YOUR ADULT DOG HAS RECENTLY BECOME TERRIFIED OF
THUNDER AND FIRECRACKERS

The best opportunity for success with this problem is desensitization. This means slowly and patiently getting your dog to adjust to the noise or noises that upset him. Purchase a tape or CD of sounds ranging from the quietest to the noisiest and start exposing him to the gentlest sounds. When your dog begins to respond without fear to one sound level praise him lavishly and motivate him with food treats, toys, or anything that he likes. Then increase the sound level to a higher volume. Work this way with all the sounds that he has the most difficulty with and repeat the same motivating techniques. This is a problem that may take quite a while. Be very patient.

IF YOUR DOG HEARS A LOUD NOISE OR YOU YELL AT HIM, HE RUNS AND HIDES UNDER THE BED AND YOU CAN'T GET HIM OUT UNTIL HE IS GOOD AND READY. YOU CANNOT FIGURE OUT WHY HE DOES THIS

There are different reasons for this problem. This could be a genetic problem, which means that maybe either his father or mother were shy. He may have had a traumatic experience as a puppy, he may have been raised in a rural area and then all of a sudden exposed to a very busy environment. He may have been scared by owners disciplining their dogs with a newspaper or making a lot of noise and verbally harsh. First, you need to identify the source of the problem; then you can give the appropriate reconditioning solution. You should never yell at your dog. Keep your dog on the leash when you are home to prevent him from going under the bed. Expose him to normal sounds in the house, such as keys dropping, doorbells ringing, pots dropping. Keep the leash and collar on and give him positive reinforcement when he doesn't respond out of fear. If he is trained and given the commands "stay" and "down," he will not run under the bed and hide. This alternative behavior instills confidence in him.

### *Fear of people*

YOUR PUPPY SEEMS AFRAID OF EVERYONE EXCEPT YOU. HE WAS FINE AT THE PET STORE WHEN YOU BOUGHT HIM. YOU DON'T KNOW HOW THIS HAPPENED

Some puppies are not properly socialized, which means they were most likely confined to a crate most of their young lives and not exposed to people in a friendly, loving way. But do not despair. The key to changing a dog's fear is socializing. Introduce your dog to as many different people in and out of your home as possible from now on. Start slowly. Talk to your dog with love but always use a soft tone of voice. Make sure everybody who meets him kneels down so that human body language is not threatening to him. Spoil him with treats, toys, or lavish expressions of affection, or all three. Most important, have more than one person handle him. Get him out in the world. Hire pet sitters or dog walkers if you must. You can turn this problem around.

Your biggest mistake was buying your dog in a pet store. Most dogs sold at pet stores are mass produced from so-called puppy mills. In most instances they have not been selectively bred for their good qualities and they have not even been bred for their bad qualities. They were just bred, period. In a puppy mill all males and females that are able to stand and mate are bred for the puppies, no matter what condition the dogs are in. You have no way of knowing what the temperament of the mother and father were like or what sicknesses were passed on to the puppies through the genes. Many of these baby dogs are like ticking time bombs waiting to go off in the future.

### YOUR DOG IS VERY SHY. YOU WANT TO TRAIN HIM BUT HE LOOKS TOO SCARED

Training and socializing is the only way you will overcome this problem. He needs to build confidence and nothing does that like dog training. It gives you and your dog the necessary structure for teaching and communicating between the two of you. All dogs and their human families need to learn the right way to live together. Think of yourself as a shy person and imagine what you would need to feel better—love, praise, and affection. You wouldn't want to be yelled at, hit, or subjected to behavior that is frightening. When training your dog, start out in a quiet, private area, and then slowly expose him to the rest of the world. Socializing your dog involves introducing him to new people and new situations. You should have great success if you take this solution seriously.

### YOUR DOG IS VERY SHY WITH PEOPLE BUT GETS ALONG WITH OTHER DOGS VERY WELL. YOU DON'T KNOW HOW TO CHANGE THIS

Chances are that your dog was raised with many dogs and bonded with them instead of with people. He may not have been exposed to many people or he may never have had the opportunity to be socialized with humans and the human environment. For puppies the critical period for optimum socialization with humans is from the first three to seven weeks of life. That is when they are best able to adapt to those around them. The dog may have been raised during this critical period, and longer, with other dogs and few humans, he therefore may be shy with people. However, it is never too late to begin the process of socializing. Begin by taking the dog everywhere, in cars, on walks, or into other homes, in order to meet as many new people as possible. New people and new situations are the way to socialize a dog. Help him to understand that most people are okay. With intensive socializing and with training you will be able to remove a lot of his fear of people.

### YOUR DOG SEEMS TO LIKE WOMEN ONLY. IT IS PUZZLING

The most obvious possibility is that the dog was raised by a woman with no man present in his life, or by a man who was abusive. In that situation men are unfamiliar and viewed with suspicion, almost like another species. Conversely, this also happens with a dog who doesn't like women because he was raised exclusively by a man. The solution is obvious. Socialize the dog intensely with many members of the opposite sex so that he will become comfortable with everyone. If the problem is not addressed properly, the dog will live with fear every time he encounters a member of the opposite sex that he is uncomfortable with. And a dog that lives with fear most of the time can become aggressive as he gets older. Many small dogs develop this problem because their owners baby them so much. Large dogs with this problem obviously can become threatening and perhaps dangerous. This problem develops when a dog is not socialized enough with people. It is not healthy for a dog or his owner to have such a limited relationship. Consider such a dog when going to a veterinarian, a professional groomer, or staying at a boarding kennel. He is bound to be extremely frightened because he doesn't know anyone but his owner.

### ALL SHY DOGS BITE

Of course not. There are different levels of shyness. Some dogs are simply timid, others are sensitive or mildly fearful but behave very sweetly. In dog behavior, a completely shy dog is one that is frightened of anyone unfamiliar and of all new situations, events, or places. A completely shy dog is one that is quite likely to bite out of fear.

## *Growling*

### WHEN YOUR DOG GROWLS, IT OFTEN LEADS TO BITING

Growling is a warning signal from your dog that he will bite if you do not stop whatever it is that is upsetting him. Because you love your dog so much, you can't imagine that he could growl at the family as well as at a stranger. Growling at somebody definitely can lead to biting, which often leads to serious injuries. You must ask yourself if you would be frightened by the same behavior from someone else's dog. If it were another dog, would you be scared that he may bite? If the answer is yes, then you have to look at this problem very seriously.

### YOU LOVE YOUR DOG VERY MUCH. BUT WHEN YOU HUG HIM AND PUT YOUR FACE CLOSE TO HIS, HE GROWLS

Be careful or you may be getting a facelift you hadn't counted on. He doesn't growl in your face because he doesn't love you. In the dog's mind, you are trying to dominate him and his growling is a warning for you to stop. If he is a fearful or shy dog, then you are probably scaring him. Either way, when a dog growls he is warning you that he will bite. You must stop this behavior immediately. Growling is aggressive behavior and totally unacceptable. First, do not hug a dog that does not like it and growls. If he does growl, you must correct this behavior with a strong "no." A leash correction is even better. Always think of the dog's behavior from the dog's point of view and imagine if somebody scared you with a hug. What would you do?

### WHEN YOUR DOG PLAYS WITH THE NEIGHBOR'S DOG, THERE IS A LOT OF AGGRESSIVE GROWLING GOING ON. IT SOUNDS LIKE IT COULD LEAD TO A DOGFIGHT

Not necessarily. It depends on the age of the dogs. If they are puppies they are probably just playing. If they are adult dogs of the opposite sex there is most likely nothing to worry about. If they are of the same sex and they are adult dogs, it could lead to a serious fight. When dogs of the same sex are younger their play behavior involves some growling that is harmless. When they reach maturity, however, they may not always get along and you must stay aware of this.

YOUR DOG LOVES TO CHEW HIS BONES AND PLAY WITH HIS TOYS, BUT WHEN YOU GET NEAR HIM, HE GROWLS AND LOOKS AGGRESSIVE. YOU GUESS YOU SHOULD JUST LEAVE HIM ALONE WHEN HE CHEWS HIS BONE

Yes, but aggressive behavior should never be tolerated. This is called possessive aggression, and if it is not corrected it will lead to other forms of aggression. Sooner or later you will get bitten. A leash correction along with a verbal correction is necessary whenever your dog behaves this way. Obedience training, of course, is the most important solution for this problem. If your dog is over one year of age and you are concerned about your safety, get help from a professional dog trainer.

YOU WOULD LIKE TO STOP YOUR DOG FROM GROWLING AT STRANGERS

You cannot, if you encourage this behavior by praising or rewarding him when he growls at a stranger. Some people believe that this behavior offers them protection. The problem here is that not all strangers are bad. Obedience training and socializing are absolute necessities to prevent your dog from biting the wrong stranger.

YOUR DOG GROWLS AT EVERYONE AND EVERYTHING. MAYBE IT'S A GENETIC PROBLEM

It probably is. As dogs can have physical problems

that are inherited, so they can have social problems as well. It is very important to get a professional evaluation from an experienced dog trainer who has dealt with aggressive behavior. You cannot change genetics, but you can modify your dog's behavior by gaining control over him. Recognizing this behavior when your dog is young could save his life. If he growls and then seriously bites someone he may have to be destroyed.

### Guilt

YOUR DOG ALWAYS LOOKS SO GUILTY WHENEVER YOU GET HOME FROM WORK. YOU SEARCH THE HOUSE TO SEE IF HE HAS DONE SOMETHING WRONG

Most likely, the first time you came home and found he had done something wrong, you dragged him to the scene of the crime, told him how bad he was, maybe hit him, pointed at him, yelled at him, got all of your frustration out, and basically terrified him. He might have chewed up the couch, had a housebreaking accident, or destroyed your favorite shoes. It really doesn't matter what he did, only how you responded to the situation. Unless you catch the dog in the act, he can't be disciplined for something he "did wrong" after the fact. The dog really has no idea what the fuss is about. So the next time you come home and you get that guilty look, it's not that he's done something wrong, it's that he's expecting some form of punishment because it seems to be associated with you coming home.

PEOPLE HAVE TOLD YOU THAT DOGS FEEL GUILTY ABOUT
THEIR BEHAVIOR

The answer to that is no. It is a human emotion, not
a dog emotion.

WHEN YOU YELL AT YOUR DOG, HE LOOKS SO SAD AND
GUILTY, IT MAKES YOU FEEL TERRIBLE. MAYBE HE IS DOING
THIS ON PURPOSE SO YOU WON'T YELL AT HIM

No, absolutely not. When you yell at your dog you
are scaring him to death. Dogs hear five times better
than humans. How would you like it if somebody
yelled directly into your ear? Think about this the next
time you yell at your dog. He's not feeling guilt, it's
fear. Your angry tone of voice creates a "guilty look."
The solution is so simple. Don't yell at your dog. Learn
how to train him.

### Jealousy

YOUR ADULT DOG, WHO HAS BEEN THE "BABY" UP UNTIL
NOW, SEEMS JEALOUS OF YOUR NEW BABY, WHO HAS BEEN
GETTING ALL THE ATTENTION LATELY

First of all, dogs do not experience jealousy, certainly not the way people experience it. It is a complex
human emotion. A problem may arise if your dog has
never been exposed to children in a meaningful way.
For all of his life he was your "baby" and now a human
baby has arrived. Some dogs will adjust to this new situation comfortably and some dogs who have personality or social problems may not. If your dog barks,
growls, or shows any sign of aggression, you should
consult a professional dog trainer or animal behavior-

ist before introducing the dog to the baby, just to be safe.

### EVERY TIME YOU PLAY WITH YOUR NEW PUPPY, THE OLDER DOG SEEMS JEALOUS AND DEMANDS ATTENTION

As stated above, the issue is not jealousy. Maybe the older dog simply wants to join in the fun and get some attention too. Some people have a tendency to think their dog feels what they would feel in a similar situation, rather than try to understand things from the dog's point of view. Dogs do not experience jealousy in the complex manner of humans. Sometimes they feel threatened, or excluded, or needy, but not necessarily jealous. When you play with a puppy it is quite likely that your dog just wants to join in the fun.

### YOUR DOG SEEMS TO BE JEALOUS EVERY TIME YOU KISS YOUR HUSBAND

Kiss your dog first and then your husband.

## Jumping fences

### YOU LOVE YOUR DOG AND GIVE HIM LOTS OF ATTENTION, BUT HE CONTINUES TO JUMP OVER YOUR FENCE

There are a number of reasons why this happens. There may be one or more female dogs in the neighborhood that are in heat. The sexual odor from a female who is in season and ready to mate is powerful and designed to attract male dogs. Although you may not notice it, the scent of a female in heat is in the air and as plain as the nose on your dog's face. His desire to jump the fence and roam may also be a sign of wanderlust, which usually happens when he comes into sexual maturity. Most dogs sooner or later want to explore; male dogs more than females. If your dog was at one time in his life a stray, he may be reverting back to his old way of life. Some dogs are hungry and want to go out scavenging for food. Perhaps something is scaring your dog, such as a persistent noise or kids that torment him. In that case he will do what he can to avoid staying in the yard. You can resolve some of these reasons by having your dog neutered; altered dogs tend to lose their desire to roam. Build a taller fence. If your dog is jumping over your fence then it is obviously too low. A six-foot fence or higher will keep him in.

### YOU'RE NOT SURE WHAT TO DO WHEN YOU CATCH YOUR DOG IN THE ACT OF JUMPING THE FENCE

Here are some recommended training solutions. Make sure your dog is wearing his training collar and a thirty-foot leash (add clothesline to a conventional leash for this). Have a friend or neighbor on the other side of the fence encouraging him to jump over. As he attempts to jump, give him a hard leash and verbal correction. Jerk the leash and say "no" in a firm tone of voice. Continue repeating the correction if he keeps trying to get over the fence. Some dogs are quite stubborn and require a stronger measure. Use a water hose when he tries to jump the fence to give him a good healthy drenching, saying "no" at the same time.

### YOUR DOG JUMPS THE FENCE WHEN YOU'RE NOT HOME

Some solutions, by necessity, must be based on prevention techniques, such as raising the height of the fence, building a chain-link dog run, making sure there is nothing in front of the fence to give the dog easy access, such as a stack of boxes or a trash can. If the dog is going over one specific area of the fence, place chicken wire on top of the fence that is slanted inward so he will not be able to pull himself over. Another solution is to place a long piece of wood on top of the fence. When he tries to jump, he will knock it down, which should startle him. If it does he won't want to jump on the fence again, at least not for a while.

### YOU THINK THAT A SEE-THROUGH FENCE WILL DETER YOUR DOG FROM JUMPING BETTER THAN A SOLID FENCE

A fence that the dog can see through will not necessarily deter him from jumping over. If he can see other dogs or cats or anything that seems more interesting than where he is, it will motivate him to jump over. Ideally, the best deterrent is a solid fence from which he cannot look out.

### YOUR DOG CONSTANTLY JUMPS OVER YOUR FENCE.

This problem can be solved with prevention. Make sure your fence is six feet or higher. If possible, provide a self-contained dog run. It should have a chain-link cover.

### YOU'VE TIED YOUR DOG IN THE BACKYARD SO HE WON'T JUMP OVER THE FENCE

It is not a good idea to tie the dog in the backyard. Although it may stop him from jumping over the fence, it may cause him to hurt himself. This also could create a barking problem, which will upset your neighbors. A better solution is to erect a clothesline trolley. This can be set up easily between the side of the house and a tree, approximately five feet off the ground. The height depends on the size of your dog. It must be high enough so that it does not interfere with his ability to move from one end of the trolley to the other but low enough so that he can lie down with ease. Run the hand loop of the leash through the clothesline and then hook the leash to the dog's collar. Do not use a training or choke collar for this; use a conventional leather or nylon collar. This will give him an improvised dog run when you confine him out-doors. The dog is then free to move about as he pleases, to the limits of your property.

### Jumping on furniture

YOU LET YOUR DOG SLEEP WITH YOU AT NIGHT AND HE KNOWS HE IS ALLOWED ONLY IN THE BED. DESPITE THIS, YOU ALWAYS FIND HIM SLEEPING ON YOUR COUCH

Obviously, he thinks he must be allowed on the couch if he's allowed on the bed. Maybe he's watching his favorite TV dog show, *Woof, It's a Dog's Life*. Who can blame him for getting on the couch? You are giving your dog a mixed message. Bed, yes. Couch, no. With most dogs it's got to be all or nothing. Either he is allowed to sleep on all of the furniture or none of it. You have to establish the rules and stick to them. This is usually a people problem. We like the warm, snuggly feeling of a dog in the bed but do not like dog fur and other debris on the furniture. Try covering the couch with chicken wire or sheets of aluminum foil when you're not at home. Why not get your dog a bed of his own? That might be the best solution possible.

WHEN YOU COME HOME FROM WORK, YOUR DOG IS ALWAYS WAITING FOR YOU BY THE DOOR, BUT YOU ALWAYS FIND HIS HAIR ON YOUR FAVORITE CHAIR. OBVIOUSLY, HE IS ON THE FURNITURE, BUT HE NEVER DOES IT WHEN YOU'RE AT HOME

This is a problem that develops if you let your dog sit next to you or on your lap while you are in your favorite chair. This makes it more of a people problem than a dog problem. Your dog associates sitting on your chair with being next to you and enjoying your love and affection. If you do not want him on the furniture you must first stop inviting him to sit with you. It is too confusing for him to figure out when he can and when he cannot sit there. Next, you need to correct him if you find him on your chair. However, you must first catch him in the act before you can correct him with a leash correction. But even if you do catch him in the act, you must not yell at him or say "bad dog" in a harsh tone of voice. Do nothing that will make him frightened of you. Try to make it unappealing to him to sit on your chair by taking a piece of chicken wire and spreading it out on the chair. You can count on him not liking it when he jumps up on the chair; it will not feel like silk. This is a self-correcting method where the dog does not associate you with punishment or harsh treatment. He will learn to stay off your chair all by himself. It is a very neat solution to an irritating problem.

He's Driving Me Crazy  249

You've spoiled your dog by allowing him to sleep on the furniture. Now you're getting new furniture and don't want him on it any longer

You have come to a wise decision. The solution here is consistency of rules plus obedience training. This is the only answer for this problem. It's never too late to change the rules if you do it properly. Remember that you *can* teach an old dog new tricks.

### *Jumping on people*

Your dog loves to jump up on people

There are many reasons for this problem. The most common being dog owners permitting their puppies and adolescent dogs to jump on them because it's cute. Once the dog grows up, though, and weighs between fifty to eighty pounds and has the energy of a young adult, it is no longer cute. By then you're stuck with the habit. This is a people problem rather than a dog problem. Other reasons for jumping range from dogs simply having excitable temperaments or expressing unbridled joy at the first sight of anyone from the family. Anyone who relates to a dog with a high-pitched, exuberant voice will excite him and get him to jump up and lick his or her face. Some people actually teach their dogs to jump on them because of their style of play. If you hold a ball or toy or food treat above your dog's head, getting him up on his hind legs to get the object, you are teaching your dog to jump.

## YOUR DOG JUMPS ON YOUR GUESTS WHEN THEY VISIT YOU. HE LOVES EVERYONE, BUT NOT EVERYONE LOVES HIM

The quickest most effective way to stop this behavior is to administer a leash correction as he begins to jump on someone. You must anticipate this behavior by having his training collar and leash on him. When he starts to jump, grab the leash with both hands and hold it a bit below your waist level. Jerk the leash sideways and slightly upward to the right. As you jerk the leash say "no" in a firm tone of voice. Return the leash to its original position in one quick motion. This should get the dog to get down immediately, with all four paws on the ground. Quickly praise him for his good response by saying "good dog." The correction stops the unwanted behavior. The praise is to let him know that getting down was the right thing. It also encourages him to stop jumping on people in the future. It is his reward and there is no such thing as too much praise. You must set up the situation for this technique when you know that people are coming over. The biggest mistake dog owners make is not having the tools for correction handy as the problem occurs. Another effective solution is teaching the dog alternative behavior. This involves dog training commands as offered in Chapter 4, "He Won't Listen to Me." For the problem of jumping on people, teach your dog the command "sit/stay." Obviously, when he is in that stationary position, he can't jump.

YOU HAVE USED LEASH CORRECTIONS TO STOP YOUR
DOG FROM JUMPING WITH GREAT SUCCESS. BUT HE STILL
JUMPS ON PEOPLE ONCE YOU TAKE THE LEASH AND
COLLAR OFF. YOU NEED ANOTHER TECHNIQUE

Another corrective technique is to use an empty
soda can with twenty pennies taped inside. As the dog
starts to jump on someone, shake the can vigorously,
which will make a loud noise, and say "no" in a firm
tone of voice. This should get the dog down. Praise
him right away. You also can use a spray bottle filled
with water as a correction device. As he jumps, squirt
him and say "no" in a firm voice. It will startle him and
discourage him from jumping in the future. Another
technique is to use a whistle. As the dog begins to
jump, blow the whistle. Because dogs have much more
sensitive hearing than humans, he will stop jumping.
Once he gets down praise him and tell him he's good.

SOME PEOPLE HAVE SUGGESTED THAT YOU KNEE YOUR
DOG IN THE CHEST WHEN HE JUMPS TO STOP THIS
BEHAVIOR

This tactic does not work. It hurts the dog and has
the potential for creating a serious injury. Never use
your body in a negative way when relating to a dog. Do
not use your knees or your hands to hurt your dog in
the belief that this is an effective way to train him. Believe it or not, some people step on their dog's back
toes to correct this problem. Where is the love and affection in that?

IT IS OKAY FOR YOUR DOG TO JUMP ON YOU, BUT NOT
ON ANYBODY ELSE

As long as you don't mind the problem and enjoy
him jumping on you, there is nothing wrong with it.
The only problem with it is when you get dressed up
and he jumps on you. If you tell him "no" because of
your nice clothes, you will confuse him. Unless your
dog can tell the difference between your dirty jeans
and a clean suit, you should consider not encouraging
this problem.

### Leash rejection

WHEN YOU TRY TO PUT A LEASH ON YOUR PUPPY HE
GOES CRAZY, LIKE A BUCKING BRONCO. HE BECOMES
SCARED AND IT MAKES EVERYONE FEEL TERRIBLE

Here is the proper way to get him used to a leash.
Use a buckled collar meant for puppies and attach a
very lightweight leash to it. You can even use heavy
string or lightweight clothesline about four feet long.
Place it on your young dog and let him drag it around
all day so that he becomes used to it. Pick up the leash
many times a day during this period of adjustment but
do it in a relaxed way and do not apply any tension to
the line. Do not attempt to control his movements
with it. Just let him drag it around. Avoid accidents by
not leaving the puppy alone with the leash or string attached. Because the puppy is unaccustomed to having
anything hanging from him, talk to him with enthusiasm and give him tender loving care. After a while he
will ignore it. He may make his adjustment in between
one and seven days. Once he is dragging the leash hap-

pily behind him, try picking it up. If he offers no resistance, substitute the string with a standard-size leather leash that is six feet long and five-eighths of an inch wide. Try walking with the dog as you gently hold the leash. If he refuses to walk, kneel down and call him to you in a happy, loving tone of voice. If he tries to bite or chew the leash, give him a mild correction by saying "no" in a firm tone of voice. Praise him immediately afterward. Once he seems to have made an adjustment to the leash in the house, try walking outdoors. It is best to begin on a soft, grassy surface. If he still resists, at least the grass will prevent his paws from painfully scraping as you gently pull him forward. A dog that refuses to walk on a leash will stay behind you. A leash-broken dog will walk closer to you, but will pull. Be patient and continue to encourage the dog to walk to you. Do not carry the dog. Maintain a positive attitude. Make your voice sound happy and keep kneeling if you have to in order to entice the dog to walk to you. Eventually he will.

## YOUR DOG IS SO SMALL, YOU CARRY HIM EVERYWHERE

You should put him down like every other dog and get a leash on him. This is absolutely necessary. If you keep carrying your puppy around you may be making him insecure and shy so that he will never walk on a leash. There are many times when he must. Most people who have small dogs love to carry them around in their arms. You never see anyone carrying a Great Dane puppy in their arms. Treat your small dog like a big dog and he will feel like a big dog.

### YOUR PUPPY TRIES TO BITE THE LEASH EVERY TIME YOU TRY TO TAKE HIM FOR A WALK

It is possible that his gums hurt from teething as his permanent teeth come in. If that's the case he will be chewing on everything and anything and needs time and patience until the process is complete, which can take weeks. Try to ease his pain with ice cubes and frozen washcloths. In the meantime, you cannot allow him to chew on the leash. Try giving him a mild leash correction and say "no" in a firm tone of voice whenever he bites down where he shouldn't. If he has not been broken in on his leash, see the first topic in this section. Another solution involves the use of alum powder (a generic product available in most pharmacies). Just add a small amount of water to a teaspoon of alum, enough to make a thick paste, and smear it on the part of the leash he is biting. It has a bitter taste and it will discourage him from chewing there.

### YOU'RE NOT SURE WHICH KIND OF LEASH AND COLLAR ARE BEST FOR WALKING YOUR DOG

We recommend a leather leash for just about all situations because it is softer on your hands, more flexible, and very reliable. It is almost impossible for a dog to break a leather leash, and you can see it wearing out before it breaks. Use a flat nylon or leather buckle collar when breaking in your dog on his leash. Do not use a metal or nylon choke collar during this breaking-in period. Once the dog has adjusted to walking on the leash with no problem, change over to a corrective or choke collar made of leather, nylon, or metal.

YOUR PUPPY SEEMS READY TO START WEARING A LEASH

You can start putting a leash and conventional flat buckle collar on him as young as eight weeks. Be certain he is always supervised when he is wearing his leash and collar; you must not allow him to hurt himself. If he is teething, he will certainly try to chew away as much of the leash as he can. Do not allow this to happen.

## Mounting

YOUR DOG TRIES TO MOUNT THE LEGS OF YOUR GUESTS

An important reason for mounting is your dog's dominant personality. It is often an assertion of higher rank in the pack; your dog is trying to demonstrate that he is the top dog. It may also be an indication of adolescence or the onset of sexual maturity. Your dog will not stop this embarrassing behavior until you make it clear that it is unacceptable. You must correct him with a firm leash correction and a firm "no." Some dogs develop extremely aggressive behavior if mounting behavior is not corrected. Neutering and spaying are highly recommended for dogs that just cannot stop. This will not prevent the problem totally, but it will make it easier to solve.

## Nipping and mouthing

YOU'VE HEARD THE TERMS "NIPPING" AND "MOUTHING," BUT YOU DON'T UNDERSTAND THE DIFFERENCE

Nipping is when your dog will take little bites of your hand, usually when he is teething or wants your attention. Mouthing is when your dog takes your entire hand or a large part of it in his mouth as if it were a play toy. Both behaviors are unacceptable and both can hurt. In either case, say "no" in a firm tone of voice when it happens and administer a leash correction if possible. Remember, you cannot administer a leash correction unless your dog is wearing a leash and choke collar.

### YOUR PUPPY KEEPS BITING YOU WITH HIS SHARP TEETH

Almost all puppies go through the stage of teething from the age of five weeks to six months. Teething causes pain and itching in the gums as the new, permanent teeth break through. It's as if you had a major toothache and the only way to ease it was to bite on something. Here are some quick solutions to keep you from being chewed up by your teething puppy. Soak six washcloths in cold water, twist them, and put them in the freezer. Give your teething puppy a frozen washcloth to chew on every two hours. The coldness will numb his gums and give him some relief. A dish of ice cubes also can help in the same way, though ice cubes will not last as long as frozen washcloths. Give your dog a leash correction when he chews inappropriately. That means you should keep the leash and collar on him when you are home. When he starts to chew on you, correct him and give him one of his toys so that he learns the difference between what he can and cannot chew. Sometimes your puppy needs a time-out from you. Place him in a wire dog crate and give him some of his favorite toys. This will make everybody happy.

WHEN YOU PLAY WITH YOUR DOG HE KEEPS BITING YOUR HANDS. ALTHOUGH HE DOES IT IN A PLAYFUL MANNER, IT DOESN'T SEEM LIKE A GOOD IDEA

When you allow your dog to bite your hands playfully you are encouraging him to mouth and bite your hands. At some point the dog is going to bite down hard and hurt you or whomever he is mouthing. Every time your dog sees a hand coming toward him to pet, stroke, feed, or medicate him, he will assume that he is allowed to bite. There are many other ways of playing with a dog. Retrieving, teaching him agility, or obedience competition are all great ways to enjoy your dog. Always use your hands for expressing love, praise, and affection, but do not allow your dog to associate these things with nipping, mouthing, or biting.

### Pulling on the leash

YOUR DOG IS SO STRONG, HE PULLS YOU DOWN THE STREET

See the sections on leash correction and heeling in Chapter 4, "He Won't Listen to Me." If you have trained your dog already, then give him the "heel" command just before you start to walk. Make many right U-turns in addition to administering leash corrections where appropriate. When teaching the command "heel" you are expected to perform a series of right U-turns when the dog pulls ahead and give him a leash correction at the same time as you say "Pappy, heel. Good dog."

### You've heard that your dog should be on your left side as you walk him

It's an old custom. When hunters used to hunt, they would carry their rifle with their right hand and keep the dogs on the left side. In addition, leash corrections are more effective when you jerk the leash to the right. It allows you more strength and control with the leash.

### Your dog pulls so hard on the leash, he starts to choke from the collar

Make sure that you are using the proper collar for training your dog. We recommend a metal choke collar, or what we refer to as a corrective collar. Measure the width around your dog's neck and add three inches to that figure for the proper size to ask for when making your purchase. The collar works only when you place it around your dog's neck properly. There is a right way and a wrong way to wear it. Here is an easy way to remember the right and the wrong way: When you put the collar on the right way it forms the letter P when the dog is facing you. In this way it will release smoothly and quickly after a corrective jerk to the side. The collar is on wrong if it forms the number 9 as you face the dog. When you correct him in this mode it will not release and slide back to its proper place after administering a corrective jerk to the side. If the collar is on incorrectly it will choke your dog. Practice placing the collar on your arm before trying it on the dog. If it releases smoothly after a jerk then you have it on correctly. It is better to experiment on your arm than your dog's neck.

## Ransacking garbage
YOUR DOG DIGS THROUGH THE GARBAGE WHETHER HE IS
HUNGRY OR NOT

A garbage digger may or may not do it because he is hungry. As we all know, people food has a better aroma than dog food. If your dog hangs around the kitchen waiting for you to give him leftovers, he has probably figured out that they are in the garbage can. A simple solution for this problem is to stop feeding your dog leftovers. Another solution is to keep the garbage can out of his reach with the lid on tight. You also can make the garbage unappetizing by sprinkling alum powder or Bitter Apple, a commercial product, over it.

YOUR DOG KEEPS GOING INTO THE BATHROOM GARBAGE

Sounds like he is very bored. First, close the bathroom door. Next exercise your bored dog or otherwise keep him occupied. Obedience training is a great relief from canine boredom.

## Running away
YOUR DOG IS ALWAYS TRYING TO RUN AWAY. YOU THINK
IT MEANS THAT HE DOESN'T LOVE YOU

It really depends on what kind of dog owner you are. If you yell at him and continually make him feel bad, he may be trying to get away from you. But assuming none of that is true, most likely he tries to run away simply because he hasn't been taught not to do it. A dog that runs away obviously hasn't been taught basic obedience commands, such as "sit" or "sit/stay," "come when called," "down," or "down/stay." When a dog runs away it may have nothing at all to do with love. He may simply need some basic obedience training.

YOUR DOG LIKES TO ROAM AROUND THE NEIGHBOR-HOOD. HE MAY JUMP OVER YOUR FENCE OR DIG HIS WAY OUT OF THE YARD JUST SO HE CAN RUN AWAY

Neutering may help this situation, but it may not necessarily solve the problem. See "Jumping fences" earlier in this chapter.

YOUR DOG LIKES TO RUN OUT AS SOON AS THE FRONT DOOR IS OPENED. YOU MUST CHASE HIM DOWN THE STREET THROUGH TRAFFIC AND STROLLING PEOPLE TO GET HIM BACK

It is important to know that when you chase your dog he may think it is a wonderful game. Sometimes running the other way and calling him will get him to chase after you. If he does, kneel down and coax him toward you with his favorite toy or food treat. It is essential to have his leash and collar ready to place around him the minute you can reach him. The next step is to learn how to prevent this from happening in the future. The most important tools for correcting this problem are two training commands. See the sections on the "sit/stay" and "down/stay" commands in Chapter 4, "He Won't Listen to Me." If you teach your dog these commands and if you employ them just before opening a door each and every time, your running away problem will come to an end. It is also important to reinforce these commands by practicing them every day until you are certain the dog will obey and not run away.

### WHEN YOU TAKE YOUR DOG OFF HIS LEASH AND TELL HIM TO COME TO YOU, HE DOESN'T LISTEN. YOU'RE AFRAID THAT HE IS GOING TO GET HIT IN TRAFFIC ONE OF THESE DAYS

The greatest mistake dog owners can make is to assume their dog will come to them when he is off his leash. This is based on the belief that the dog will listen to them simply because he loves them. But love has nothing to do with teaching off-leash training. A dog that has been trained off his leash is like a college graduate, but he must first go through the equivalent of high school with basic obedience training. So if you want your dog to listen to you when he is off his leash, he has to be perfectly trained on his leash. See the section "Come When Called" in Chapter 4, "He Won't Listen to Me," which involves the use of a six-foot leash. This is what is required for on-leash training. Off-leash training is highly specialized and beyond the scope of this book. Teaching your dog to come when called off-leash requires training techniques using a thirty-foot leash, a fifty-foot light clothesline, and a training tab, which is the loop of the leash and a snap only. To teach your dog off-leash responses you will need help from a professional trainer or from a training manual specializing in this work.

### Spite

YOU THINK YOUR DOG DOES BAD THINGS JUST FOR SPITE,
JUST TO GET BACK AT YOU

Dogs are not spiteful. That is an emotion experienced by humans. It is important to understand that your dog is not a human. He's a dog. When dogs do bad things they are not really bad, they are behavior problems, or social problems, or normal puppy problems. As a matter of fact, most of the troubling behavior of dogs is only problematic within the human environment. In a natural setting they are normal and to be expected, such as so-called housebreaking accidents.

YOU THINK YOUR DOG IS SPITEFUL BECAUSE EVERY TIME
YOU LEAVE HE GOES TO THE BATHROOM IN THE HOUSE

This behavior has nothing to do with spite. Your dog is probably not housebroken, or is improperly confined, or is on an improper feeding-walking schedule, or maybe has a favorite spot he wants to continue using as a toilet. None of these things have to do with spite, they have to do with housebreaking issues. You must figure out why your dog is doing these things and then find the proper solution.

### Stealing food

WHENEVER YOU LEAVE THE KITCHEN, EVEN FOR JUST A
MINUTE, YOUR DOG JUMPS UP ON THE COUNTER AND
STEALS WHATEVER FOOD HE CAN FIND

Your dog surely loves your cooking. He does this because it smells good and it probably tastes good too.

The truth is that many dogs would eat all day long if you let them. Here is a very quick solution: Don't leave your dog alone in the kitchen. How's that for great dog training advice?

### YOUR DOG HAS BEEN STEALING FOOD FROM YOUR TABLE OR FROM THE GARBAGE

He may be hungry because he is not being fed enough food. Check with your veterinarian. If he steals food from your kitchen, it is probably because your food always smells better than his dog food.

### YOU FEED YOUR DOG LEFTOVERS AS A WAY OF DISCOURAGING HIM FROM STEALING FOOD

This is not a good idea. In fact, when you feed your dog leftovers from the table you are actually teaching him to beg, and, ironically, encouraging him to steal food.

# Recommended Reading List

## BEHAVIOR

Beaver, Bonnie V. and Ray Kersey. *Canine Behavior: A Guide for Veterinarians.* Philadelphia: Saunders, 1998.

Bergman, Goran. *Why Does Your Dog Do That?* New York: Howell Book House, 1971.

Caras, Roger A. *A Dog Is Listening.* New York: Simon & Schuster, 1993.

Darwin, Charles. *The Expression of the Emotions in Man and Animals.* Chicago: University of Chicago Press, 1965.

Ewer, R. F. *The Carnivores.* Ithaca, New York: Cornell University Press, 1973.

Fox, Michael W. *Behavior of Wolves, Dogs and Related Canids*. New York: Harper & Row, 1971.

Lorenz, Konrad. *Man Meets Dog*. New York: Penguin, 1964.

Milani, Myrna M. *The Body Language and Emotion of Dogs*. New York: William Morrow & Co., 1993.

Pfaffenberger, Clarence. *The New Knowledge of Dog Behavior*. New York: Howell Book House, 1963.

Scott, John Paul and John L. Fuller. *Genetics and the Social Behavior of the Dog: The Classic Study*. Chicago: University of Chicago Press, 1998.

Tinbergen, N. *The Study of Instinct*. New York and Oxford: Oxford University Press, 1951, 1969.

Tortora, Daniel, Ph.D. *Help! This Animal Is Driving Me Crazy*. Chicago: Playboy Press, 1977.

Trumler, Eberhard. *Your Dog and You*. New York: Seabury Press, 1973.

## DOG TRAINING, CARE, AND HEALTH

American Kennel Club. *The Complete Dog Book*. 19th Ed., rev. New York: Howell Book House, 1997.

Carlson, Delbert G., D.V.M. and James M. Giffin, M.D. *Dog Owner's Home Veterinary Handbook*. New York: Howell Book House, 1992.

Dibra, Bash and Ann Crenshaw. *Dogspeak: How to Learn It, Speak It, Use It to Develop a Happy, Healthy Well-Behaved Dog*. New York: Simon & Schuster, 1999.

Garvey, Michael S., D.V.M., Ann E. Hohenhaus, D.V.M., Katherine A. Houpt, D.V.M., John E. Pinckney, D.V.M., Melissa S. Wallace, D.V.M., and Elizabeth Randolph. *The Veterinarian's Guide to Your Dog's Symptoms*. New York: Villard, 1999.

Hodgson, Sarah. *The Complete Idiot's Guide to Choosing, Training, and Raising a Dog*. New York: Alpha Books, 1996.

_____, *Dog Perfect: The User-friendly Guide to a Well-Behaved Dog*. New York: Howell Book House, 1995.

Kilcommons, Brian and Sarah Wilson, *Childproofing Your Dog: A Complete Guide to Preparing Your Dog for the Children in Your Family*. New York: Warner Books, 1994.

_____. *Good Owners, Great Dogs*. Training. New York: Warner Books, 1992.

Kalstone, Shirlee. *How to Housebreak Your Dog in 7 Days*. New York: Bantam, 1984.

Monks of New Skete. *How to Be Your Dog's Best Friend: A Training Manual for Dog Owners*. Boston: Little, Brown, 1978.

_____. *The Art of Raising a Puppy*. Boston: Little, Brown, 1991.

Margolis, Matthew and Catherine Swan. *The Dog In Your Life*. New York: Vintage Books, 1979.

Siegal, Mordecai, Faculty and Staff, School of Veterinary Medicine, University of California, Davis. *UC-DAVIS School of Veterinary Medicine Book of Dogs: A Complete Medical Reference Guide for Dogs and Puppies*. New York: HarperCollins, 1995.

Siegal, Mordecai. *Understanding the Dog You Love: A Guide to Preventing and Solving Behavior Problems in Your Dog*. New York: Berkley Books, 1994.

Siegal, Mordecai and Matthew Margolis. *Good Dog,*

*Bad Dog,* rev. ed. Training. New York: Henry Holt, 1991.

_____. *Grrr: The Complete Guide to Understanding and Preventing Aggressive Behavior in Dogs.* Boston: Little, Brown, 2000.

_____. *I Just Got A Puppy, What Do I Do?* Training and Care. New York: Fireside, 1992.

_____. *The Ultimate Guide to Dog Training.* New York: Fireside, 1998.

_____. *When Good Dogs Do Bad Things.* Boston: Little, Brown, 1986.

Spadafori, Gina. *Dogs For Dummies.* Dog Care. Foster City, CA: IDG Books Worldwide, 1996.

United States Air Force. *Military Working Dog Program.* Training. Air Force Manual 125-5, Volume 1. Department of the Air Force, 1973.

Woodhouse, Barbara. *No Bad Dogs: The Woodhouse Way.* New York: Simon & Schuster, 1984.

## Choosing A Dog

Kilcommons, Brian and Matthew J. Costello. *Mutts, America's Dogs: A Guide to Choosing, Loving and Living with Our Most Popular Canine.* New York: Warner Books, 1996.

Kilcommons, Brian and Sarah Wilson. *Paws to Consider: Choosing the Right Dog for You and Your Family.* New York: Warner Books, 1999.

Milani, Myrna M. *DogSmart: The Ultimate Guide to Finding the Dog You Want and Keeping the Dog You Find.* NTC Publishing Group, 1997.

Siegal, Mordecai. *Choosing the Perfect Dog for You and Your Family.* Chicago: Contemporary Books, 1994.

Tortora, Daniel F. *The Right Dog For You: Choosing a breed that matches your personality, family and lifestyle.* New York: Simon & Schuster, 1983.

Welton, Michele. *Your Purebred Puppy: A Buyer's Guide.* 2nd ed. New York: Henry Holt, 2000.

Wilcox, Bonnie, D.V.M. and Chris Walkowicz. *The Atlas of Dog Breeds of the World. The most comprehensive fully illustrated volume on dogs ever published.* Neptune City, NJ: t.f.h. Publications, 1989.

Walkowicz, Chris. *The Perfect Match: A Dog Buyer's Guide.* New York: Howell Book House, 1996.

## SPECIAL INTERESTS AND READING FOR PLEASURE

Caras, Roger A. (Essays) and Shel Secunda (Photographs). *The Bond: People and Their Animals.* New York: Simon & Schuster Editions, 1997.

Caras, Roger A. *The New Roger Caras Treasury of Great Dog Stories.* Arrowwood, 1998.

Clark, Anne Rogers and Andrew H. Brace. *The International Encyclopedia of Dogs.* New York: Howell Book House, 1995.

Cooper, Paulette and Paul Noble. *277 Secrets Your Dog Wants You To Know: A Doggie Bag of Unusual and Useful Information.* Berkley, CA: Ten Speed Press, 1995.

Coren, Stanley. *The Intelligence of Dogs: Canine Consciousness and Capabilities.* New York: Free Press, 1994.

Eames, Ed and Toni Eames. *Partners in Independence. A Success Story of Dogs and the Disabled.* New York: Howell Book House, 1997.

Gaffney, Donna A. *The Seasons of Grief: Helping Your*

*Children Grow Through Loss*. New York: New American Library, 1988.

Gavriele-Gold, Joel. *When Pets Come Between Partners: What to Do When a Pet Threatens Your Relationship*. New York: Howell Book House, 2000.

Kohl, Sam and Jim Malady (Artist). *All-Breed Dog Grooming Guide*. Pet Smart, 1987.

Levinson, Boris M., Ph.D. *Pets and Human Development*. Springfield, IL: Charles C. Thomas, Publisher, 1972.

_____. *Pet-Oriented Child Psychotherapy*. Springfield, IL: Charles C. Thomas, Publisher, 1969.

Milani, Myrna, D.V.M. and Jerry Dorsman. *Preparing for the Loss of Your Pet*. Prima Communications, 1998.

Morris, Desmond. *Dogwatching*. New York: Crown, 1986.

Morrow, Laurie. *Cold Noses and Warm Hearts: Beloved Dog Stories by Great Authors*. Willow Creek Press, 1996.

Sichel, Elaine. Photographs by Sumner W. Fowler. *Circles of Compassion: A Collection of Humane Words and Work*. Sebastopol, CA: Voice & Vision Publishing, 1995.

Siegal, Mordecai and Matthew Margolis. *Woof! The Funny and Fabulous Trials and Tribulations of 25 Years as a Dog Trainer*. New York: Crown, 1994.

Thomas, Elizabeth Marshall. *The Social Lives of Dogs: The Grace of Canine Company*. New York: Simon & Schuster, 2000.

Vanacore, Connie. *Dog Showing: An Owner's Guide*. New York: Howell Book House, 1990.

Wilcox, Bonnie, D.V.M. and Chris Walkowicz. *Old Dogs, Old Friends: Enjoying Your Older Dog.* New York: Howell Book House, 1991.